GARDEN STATE
WINERIES
GUIDE

BART JACKSON

TRAVEL
917.49
JAC
2011

OTHER BOOKS BY THE WINE APPRECIATION GUILD

"The Best Wine Publisher in the US."
—Edward Cointreau, Gourmand World Cookbook Award

Africa Uncorked, John and Erica Platter (ISBN 1-891267-52-3)

Armagnac, Charles Neal (ISBN 1-891267-20-5)

Atlas of Italian Spumanti, Zanfi (ISBN 978-8-864030-36-4)

The Bartender's Black Book, 9th ed. Stephen Kittredge Cunningham (ISBN 1-934259-17-9)

Benefits of Moderate Drinking, Gene Ford (ISBN 0-932664-60-1)

Biodynamic Wine Demystified, Nicholas Joly (ISBN 978-1-934259-02-3)

California Brandy Drinks, Malcom R. Hebert (ISBN 0-932664-21-0)

California Wine Drinks, William I. Kaufman (ISBN 0-932664-19-9)

Champagne & Sparkling Wine Guide, Tom Stevenson (ISBN 1-891267-41-8)

The Champagne Cookbook, Malcolm R. Herbert (ISBN 1-891267-70-1)

Chancers & Visionaries, Stewart (ISBN 978-1-869620-70-7)

Cheese, Gabriella Ganugi (ISBN 1-891267-69-8)

Chile the Art of Wine, Sara Matthews (ISBN 1-891267-73-7)

Chilean Wine Heritage, Rodrigo Alvarado (ISBN 1-891267-80-9)

Chow! Venice, Shannon Essa and Ruth Edenbaum (ISBN 1-934259-00-4)

The Commonsense Book of Wine, Leon D. Adams (ISBN 0-932664-76-8)

Concepts in Wine Chemistry, Yair Margalit (ISBN 1-891267-74-4)

Concepts in Wine Technology, Yair Margalit (ISBN 1-891267-51-5)

Desert Island Wine, Miles Lambert-Gocs (ISBN 978-1934259-01-6)

El Vino una Pasion, Gil (ISBN 9789879671729)

Encyclopedia of American Wine, William I. Kaurman (ISBN 0-932664-39-3)

Epicurean Recipes of California Winemakers, Malcom Hebert (ISBN 0-932664-00-8)

Essential Guide to South African Wine, 2nd Ed., Elmari Swart (ISBN 978-0-980274-23-0)

Favorite Recipes of California Winemakers, (ISBN 0-932664-03-2)

Fine Wine in Food, Patricia Ballard (ISBN 0-932664-56-3)

Food & Wine Lovers' Guide to Portugal, Metcalfe and McWhirter (ISBN 095-57069-0-4)

The French Paradox, Gene Ford (ISBN 0-932664-81-4)

Garden State Wineries Guide, Jackson (ISBN 978-1-934259-57-3)

Ghost Wineries of the Napa Valley, Irene Whitford Haynes (ISBN 0-932664-90-3)

The Global Encyclopedia of Wine, Edited by Peter Forrestal (ISBN 1-891267-38-8)

Good Wine, Bad Language, Great Vineyards: Australia (ISBN 0977514722)

Good Wine, Bad Language, Great Vineyards: New Zealand (ISBN 0-977514-72-2)

Grands Crus of Bordeaux, Hans Walraven (ISBN 0-932664-94-6)

Grape Man of Texas, McLeRoy and Renfro (ISBN 1-934259-04-7)

Grappa, Ove Boudin (ISBN 91-633-1351-0)

Greek Salad, Mile Lambert-Gocs (ISBN 1-189267-82-5)

Harry Waugh's Wine Diary, Harry Waugh (ISBN 0-932664-53-9)

Hospice de Beaune, Gotti (ISBN 978-2-35-156-049-5)

How and Why to Build a Wine Cellar, Richard Gold (ISBN 978-1-891267-00-0)

How to Import Wine, Gray (ISBN 978-1-934259-61-0)

Hungary, David Copp (ISBN 963-86759-6-9)

I Supertuscan, Carlo Gambi (ISBN 88-88482-40-7)

Icon: Art of the Wine Label, Jeffrey Caldewey and Chuck House (ISBN 1-891267-30-2)

Imagery: Art for Wine, Bob Nugent (ISBN 1-891267-30-2)

In Celebration of Wine and Life, Richard R. Lamb and Ernest Mittelberger, (ISBN 0-932664-13-X)

Journey Among the Great Wines of Sicily, Carlo Gambi (ISBN 88-88482-10-5)

Lombardia, Zanfi (ISBN 978-8-888482-98-9)

Making Sense of Wine Tasting, Alan Young (ISBN 978-1-891267-03-1)

Napa Wine: A History, Charles L. Sullivan (ISBN 1-891267-07-8)

New Adventures in Wine Cookery (ISBN 1-891267-71-X)

The New Italy, Daniele Cernelli and Marco Sabellico (ISBN 1-891267-32-9)

New Wines of Spain, Tony Lord (ISBN 0-932664-59-8)

Northern Wine Works, 2nd ed. Thomas A. Plocher (ISBN 1-934259-18-7)

Olive Oil, Leonardo Romanelli (ISBN 1-891267-55-8)

Oregon Eco-Friendly Wine, Clive Michelsen (ISBN 91-975326-4-9)

Pasta, Fabrizio Ungaro (ISBN 1-891267-56-6)

Piedmont, Carlo Gambi (ISBN 88-88482-43-1)

Pleasures of the Canary Islands, Ann and Larry Walker (ISBN 0-932664-75-X)

Po Folks Favorite Recipes, William I. Kaufman (ISBN 0-932664-50-4)

Pocket Encyclopedia of American Wine, Northwest, William I. Kaufman (ISBN 0-932664-58-X)

Pocket Encyclopedia of California Wine, William I. Kaufman (ISBN 0-932664-42-3)

Portugal's Wines & Wine Makers, New Revised Edition, Richard Mason (ISBN 1-891267-01-9)

Prosciutto, Carla Bardi (ISBN 1-891267-54-X)

Red & White, Max Allen (ISBN 1-891267-37-X)

Rhone Renaissance, Remington Norman (ISBN 0-932664-95-4)

Rich,Rare & Red, Ben Howkins (ISBN 1-891267-63-9)

Rum, Dave Broom (ISBN 1-891267-62-0)

Sauternes, Jeffrey Benson and Alastair McKenzie (ISBN 0-856673-60-9)

The Science of Healthy Drinking, Gene Ford (ISBN 1-891267-47-7)

Secrets of Chilean Cuisine, Robert Marin (ISBN 956-316-014-2)

Secrets of Patagonian Barbecue, Robert Marin (956-316-015-0)

Secrets of Peruvian Cuisine, Emilio Peschiera (956-8077-71-5)

Swallow This, Phillips (ISBN 978-0-615302-09-6)

The Taste of Wine, Emile Peynaud (ISBN 0-932664-64-4)

Tasting & Grading Wine, Clive Michelsen (ISBN 9-197532-60-6)

Terroir, James E. Wilson (ISBN 1-891267-22-1)

Tokaj, David Copp (ISBN 963-87524-3-2)

Tokaji Wine, Lambert-Gocs (ISBN 978-1-934259-49-8)

Tuscany, Zanfi (ISBN 9788864030050)

Understanding Wine Technology, 2nd Ed.,David Bird (ISBN 978-1-934259-60-3)

The University Wine Course, Marian Baldy (ISBN 0-932664-69-5)

Veneto, Zanfi (ISBN 978-8-888482-80-4)

Vine Lines, Wine Cartoons, Judy Valon (ISBN 978-1-891267-93-2)

What Price Bordeaux , Lewin (ISBN 978-1-934-25-9)

White Burgundy, Christopher Fielden (ISBN 0-932664-62-8)

The Wine Buyer's Record Book, Ralph Steadman (ISBN 0-932664-98-9)

Wine Faults, Hudelson, (ISBN 978-1-934258-63-4)

Wine, Food & the Good Life, Arlene Mueller and Dorothy Indelicato (ISBN 0-932664-85-0)

A Wine Growers' Guide, Philip M. Wagner (ISBN 0-932664-92-X)

Wine Heritage, Dick Rosano (ISBN 1-891267-13-2)

Wine in Everyday Cooking, Patricia Ballard ((ISBN 0-932664-45-8)

Wine is a Passion, Gil (ISBN 978-9-879671-72-6)

Wine Investment for Portfolio Diversification, Mahesh Kumar (ISBN 1-891267-84-1)

Wine Lovers Cookbook, Malcolm R. Herbert (ISBN 0-932664-82-2)

Wine Marketing & Sales, 2nd Ed., Paul Wagner, Janeen Olsen, Liz Thach (ISBN 978-1-934259-25-2)

Wine Myths & Reality, (ISBN 978-1-934259-51-1)

Winery Technology & Operations, Yair Margalit (ISBN 0-932664-66-0)

The Wines of Baja California, Ralph Amey (ISBN 1-891267-65-5)

The Wines of France, Clive Coates (ISBN 1-891267-14-0)

Woody's Liquid Kitchen, Hayden Wood (ISBN 0-975212-39-7)

World Encyclopedia of Champagne & Sparkling Wine, Tom Stevenson (ISBN 1-891267-61-2)

Zinfandel, Cathleen Francisco (ISBN 1-891267-15-9)

GARDEN STATE
WINERIES
GUIDE

BART JACKSON

THE WINE APPRECIATION GUILD
SAN FRANCISCO

The Wine Appreciation Guild
360 Swift Avenue
South San Francisco , CA 94080
(650) 866-3020
www.wineappreciation.com

Book Design: Diane Spencer Hume

Library of Congress Cataloging-in-Publication Data

Jackson, Bart, 1948-

Garden state wineries guide / Bart Jackson.

p. cm.

Includes index.

ISBN 978-1-934259-57-3

1. Wine and wine making-- New Jersey . 2. Wineries-- New Jersey --Guidebooks.
3. Vineyards-- New Jersey --Guidebooks. 4. New Jersey --Guidebooks. I. Title.

TP557.J33 2011
663'.2--dc22
2011004130

TABLE OF CONTENTS

Photographs

Photographs on pages 21–27 by Mari Small, The Small Agency.

ACKNOWLEDGMENTS

I t is that brave and hard laboring group of people—the winegrowers of the Garden State—who have really made this book possible. Their dedication to the excellence of their crop and the passion of their craft has created a revolution in New Jersey wines.

Secondly, I want to acknowledge the blessed, life long of aid of my wife, Lorraine, who not only edits her husband's works, she edits him.

Special praise is truly deserved by Carol Ezzo who patiently performed the multitudinous fact checking for this volume with her own homespun personal charm and astounding attention to detail.

Many thanks also to international wine experts Gary Pavlis and Anthony Fisher for contributing their renowned expertise which will better help readers appreciate the many joys of New Jersey wine and wineries.

Thanks also for the sparks from Louis Caracciolo and Pravin Philip who revealed to me the real need for this book.

Finally, kudos to publisher/editor/mentor Bryan Imelli and the Wine Appreciation Guild for their continued belief in me, this book and the enrichment it may provide to those who partake.

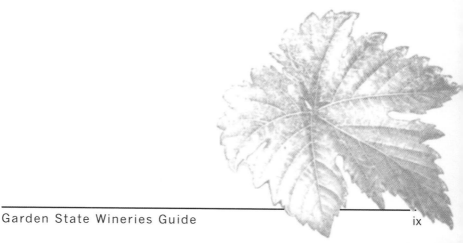

FOREWORD

GARDEN STATE WINES AND VINEYARDS

I first experienced a New Jersey produced wine in 1984. I had just finished my Ph.D. at Rutgers University and went down to Atlantic County to interview for the county agricultural agent position. After a grueling interrogation by university faculty and local farmers I decided to stop at Tomasello Winery in Hammonton. I had noticed their sign on the way down to the interview and was enthused by the prospect of working in a county that actually had a winery in it, having never visited a New Jersey winery. I met the owner, Charles Tomasello, known as Doc, enjoyed his company, tasted and bought a couple bottles of his wine, and the rest, as they say, is history.

Well I got the job and started in the summer of '84 and it turns out that the timing was right for a long and successful relationship with the New Jersey Wine Industry. The New Jersey Farm Winery Law had just been passed in 1981 and an explosion of grape growing and winery growth was about to take place. Before this law was passed, the number of wineries in the state was limited to one for every million residents, so only seven wineries could exist. This was a law that was established during Prohibition. With the passage of the Farm Winery Act, anyone with 3 acres and at least 1,200 vines could apply for a winery license. What the law really was saying was that if one grew and used grapes from New Jersey they could start a winery. What I didn't realize at the time was the positive effect this would have on the growth of the state's wine industry. The number of wineries doubled in five years and as I write, there are 54 licensed wineries in New Jersey.

During the twenty-five years that I have been involved with this industry I have seen a dramatic transformation of wine style and quality. There is no doubt that our wines in the early 1980's reflected the tastes of the wine drinking public at that time. Knowing where we are now it is almost hard to believe that the overwhelming majority of wines produced back then were sweet and usually produced from Native American varieties such as Concord, Niagara, and Delaware. But along came a few mavericks that paved the way for a renaissance within the industry. Before the '80's no one believed New Jersey could grow the classic European grape varieties that are known to make the greatest wines in the world but these mavericks weren't going to go with the status quo. Either they knew something the rest of didn't know or their thirst for something better drove them to try the impossible. In 1986 Dr. Dan Vernon of Tewksbury Wine Cellars won the Governor's Cup for the best wine entered in the New Jersey Wine Competition for a 1984 Riesling.

Wine writers were astounded, as was anyone who following the Jersey wine industry. It was a beautiful wine, easily as good as anything they were making in the Finger Lakes Region of New York but it was also very reminiscent of a good Kabinett of Germany. And it turned out that this was not a fluke. The next three Governor's Cup wines in '87, '88, and '89 were also made from Vitis vinifera grapes and were omens of great things to come.

In 1987 the top wine was a 1985 Cabernet Sauvignon from Alba Vineyards. The co-owner and operator, Rudy Marchesi, grew up in New Jersey and had watched his Italian grandparents make wine. Rudy studied winemaking in California and at first made wine in his garage. He won numerous awards for his wines in amateur competitions and so he began planting grapes and opened the winery in 1983. Alba was to become one of the major players in the quest for national recognition for the Jersey wine industry. I opened my last bottle of that '85 Cabernet a few years ago and it still was a magnificent wine, showing its age now but a hint of black cherry fruit remained as well as a complexity few had dreamed was possible when this wine was produced.

A true maverick won the 1988 Governor's cup. Frank Salek was the first in New Jersey to plant a vineyard of exclusively European grapes. At that time, he was a professor with the Newark Institute of Technology and was the consummate scientist. Whenever I would visit his house in Atlantic County his kitchen table would be covered with every grape and wine book ever published. He read everything and tried everything and in 1988 he won the competition with a 1986 Pinot Noir! Yes, Pinot Noir in New Jersey. Frank won the Governor's Cup five times and still produces classic vinifera wines today.

The last maverick I must mention was Klaus Schreiber of the now defunct King's Road Vineyard. He comes to mind because I tasted his 1989 Governor's Cup winner only last month. The wine was a 1987 Riesling and at 23 years old it was glorious. I had purchased a case after he won and this was my last bottle. Though things didn't work out at King's Road, Klaus felt that northern New Jersey was an excellent place for Riesling. He couldn't have been more right as a Riesling produced by Alba Vineyards was recently chosen as the best in North American in a prestigious national wine competition.

By the late '80s I was chairing the annual New Jersey Wine Competition and visiting the wineries regularly as part of my duties as a county agent with Rutgers Cooperative Extension. This gave me the opportunity to keep my finger on the pulse of the industry as well as contribute to the change whenever possible. I could see the change that was happening. I could taste the quality that was being produced but the Jersey wine industry was still not getting the recognition that it deserved.

People who drink wine, and even those that don't, assume all good wine comes from France, Italy, Germany and maybe California. But it is a funny thing; it is always hard to believe that it is possible for something to be great when it is produced in your own backyard. I'm not really sure why this is the case. Newspapers in this state routinely run articles on the progress the industry has made including the numerous awards that New Jersey wines win in national competitions, even beating out California wines.

In fact, as I'm writing this forward, the *Philadelphia Inquirer* is reporting that Alba and another upstart winery called Sharrott received three Gold medals in

---

the *San Francisco Chronicle* Wine Competition. But still, even though Jersey is the fifth largest consumer of wine per capita, only one percent of the wine consumed is produced in our state.

I recently decided to address this problem. As it is assumed by most that the best wines are made in France, I conducted a tasting in which New Jersey wines would be pitted against their French counterparts. The tasting was a blind tasting which means that the judges had no idea who produced the wine they were judging. I put five Chardonnays from New Jersey against five Chardonnays made in Burgundy France and five Cabernets from Jersey against five Cabernets made in Bordeaux France. The judges were all highly qualified and truth be told, most had wine cellars with the majority of bottles coming from France.

The results were astonishing. In both the case of the Chardonnay and the Cabernet wines, the Jersey wines scored higher than their French counterparts. Now it should be stated that all of these wines were comparably priced so there were no $400 bottles of Burgundy or Bordeaux in the competition. But I did this for a reason. When the average consumer goes into a wine shop, they do not ask for the best Chardonnay in the store regardless of the price. Most of us go in knowing how much we want to spend and we hope to get as good a wine as possible at that price. My tasting shows that at a modest price, you will get a better wine from New Jersey than from France. If every wine drinker understood this the bias against New Jersey wine would soon disappear.

Finally, I must close with two other important facts that may be important to the reader of this *Garden State Wineries Guide.* The range of wines produced in New Jersey is probably wider than anywhere else. Yes we have Cabernet, Chardonnay, Pinot Noir and Pinot Grigio, but we also have blueberry, cranberry, apple and dandelion as well as a host of others to tempt your palate. I firmly believe that New Jersey produces a wine that you will love, you just have to go and find it and that is half the fun. Lastly, the growth of vineyards and wineries in our state has saved many farms and preserved open space. Many a farm growing something that became unprofitable was nearly forced to sell to development but instead turned to grapes and wine. In effect, this industry is keeping the garden in the Garden State.

—Gary C. Pavlis, Ph.D.
Rutgers University
Former President of the American Wine Society

INTRODUCTION

T oday, few of us have the opportunity to behold and appreciate the farmer's exertions and expertise. Our pantries and ice boxes stand stuffed with food products processed far away, by people we will never meet. Visiting our local winery affords us a much-needed chance to reestablish that connection with the food we drink, and the individual farmer who brings it to our hands. Perhaps this is why so many people take their children to this most wholesome of experiences.

In traipsing around the wineries across our Garden State, and intermittently wineries of about seventy countries around the globe, my good wife Lorraine and I have enjoyed a universal human warmth. The shared delight that unifies vineyard labor and final taste; the mutual flow of generosity and appreciation - these are hallmarks of wineries everywhere, transcending all cultures. Granted, the winery is a place of business, but entering a tasting room, what we invariably discover, soothes the soul. How wise that the mighty traders of ancient Greece held no god of perfunctory commerce, but placed Dionysus, deity of the mystical experience of wine, proudly among their Blessed Twelve.

Increasingly, New Jersey vintages and wineries are taking a greater share in this wine adventure. Shaking off the less-than-stellar reputation, which has besieged them for decades, Garden State vintners and winemakers have exploded in number, as their products have blossomed in quality and variety. Today, ours is the six highest wine-producing state in the nation, and, by most surveys, number one in the amount imbibed.

Because of the lay of her land, as well as the high cost of her real estate, New Jersey's grape farms are small. Thus have farms always been in the Garden State. For the would-be winemaker, this offers a natural advantage. One family can stake out and farm thirty acres of wine grapes, and with a little temporary help, make a fine living for themselves. In fact, the lure of the family-run business with fair profit potential has made wineries the fastest growing agricultural business in the state.

Likewise, you, the wine lover, also benefit from these Jersey-size farms. Garden State wineries can be, and indeed are, very flexible in their selection of vinifera. Unlike the huge wineries which are petrified by their own size, nearly all our state's winemakers are planning to experiment with a few more acres of this or that grape. A quick view at this guide's winery and vinicultural maps shows how grape-friendly every Jersey nook is. The enormity and breadth of our "Common Jersey Grapes" list in the back may surprise even some veteran experts. So in your quest for sublime wines, New Jersey offers rich hunting grounds.

As you cleanse your palate and take up your glass, allow us to pass on a few winery-visiting guideposts which have served my wife and me on our treks. The

---

best wine in the world, of course, is the wine you like the best. (You'll read that gospel several times in these pages.) Not price, age, origin, nor the opinions of some pundit's personal preferences can dictate over your palate. That's part of wine's wonder. There are many truly fine wines in New Jersey that have in blind taste tests totally blown away the best of California and France. But with each sample, you alone are the ultimate judge. So explore, and seek out those several wines that best please you, being led by your palate alone.

At the same time, avoid falling into a rut of likes or dislikes. Often, as we walk toward the door of a new, untried winery, Lorraine likes to chant her little ditty:

> Please to leave your bias and snobbery at the door
> And you'll taste a vintage besting what you've ever had before.

Wise woman. After years of sipping, and hastily spitting, leadenly oaked Chardonnays, I had convinced myself that I loathed the grape. Finally on researching this book, I discovered many New Jersey vintners presenting me with a lighter, more food-friendly Chardonnay that shattered my old prejudice. Great wines are made both in the vineyard - and within the winery.

No Garden State vintages suffer more of this palate prejudice than our non-grape, fruit wines. Deeming them as lowly, vast numbers of veteran oenophiles deny themselves the true pleasures pressed from blueberry, apple, peach, and pear. Every winegrowing culture presents a substantial selection of sweeter wines to meet popular need. Because of her myriad small fruit farms, New Jersey answers this call for sweet with her fruit wines. The variety and quality of these fruit wines, one would be hard pressed to match outside our borders. They are well worthy of your experimentation. (In our own hobby vineyard, those surplus pears we have occasionally harvested and brought to vat, have frankly amazed us with their delicious results.)

Another experience-taught tip is to take your time. Wine, like romance, is not to be rushed. At the end of each winery listed in this guide, we have suggested others nearby. Some are official Garden State Winegrowers trails, (see www.newjerseywines.com), others are simply commonly taken routes. Laid out mostly in groupings of three or four, each trail makes a nice day's wine outing, with minimal driving.

Of course, each of us has his own pace that brings the utmost fulfillment, like browsing a museum or climbing a mountain. But if you seek to amble, rather than march forth in conquest intent on "doing" every winery in the state, your soul, palate, and liver will thank you. One of the great blessings of New Jersey is its enormous diversity. Whether you are watching the horseshoe crab migrations at Cape May, hiking the Appalachian Trail, paddling the Pine Barrens streams, or viewing historic reenactments in Trenton, there's a winery nearby to round out the day's discoveries. In the written "Descriptions," we mention a few such side adventures. Winery websites offer others, and by chatting with the owner at his winery, you may learn still more.

We are also fortunate that so many New Jersey vineyards are connected to working farms with several crops, animals, and home made goodies for the picnic. Both families and groups should check the "Facilities" section of each winery for accommodations and dining offerings.

As to when to visit, please take note of "The Year in Wine," which briefly outlines some of the more spectacular and intriguing festivals held on site. Of course, to take in the greatest panoply of wine offerings, be sure attend at least one New Jersey Wine Growers Association Festival where twenty to thirty of the state's vineyards display their wares amidst music and a wonderfully bizarre range of entertainment. Also, note the winery's "Events" and "Harvest Season" which give dates of everything from barefoot grape stomping to barrel-tasting fine reserves.

Finding yourself amidst a sea of glistening bottles on some new winery's gleaming counter can be a daunting experience. Traditionalists may go for those recently having achieved awards. Or you might begin sampling the "Owner's Most Prized and Favored Wines" list. These are those which the owners most prefer themselves and/or are most anxious for you to try. Those confining their quest to a few specific grapes might best be guided by each profile's "Vineyard Production" section.

Finally, one additional reward comes from launching your own Garden State winery foray. Great as the wine itself, equal to discovering furtive enchantments within the state, are the encounters with the winery owners themselves. As mentioned, New Jersey wineries are small and typically family owned. Owners are those rare few who have carved out their own life, on their own terms, and, for today at least, it is succeeding. They embody America's entrepreneurial idea, seen without the maudlin glasses of nostalgia.

Many have come to this trade as multigenerational farmers, seeking to save their land by planting the ultimate cash crop. Others, coming as corporate refugees, are seeking a way to save personal sanity and soul.

Whatever brought them here, they are laborers. Hard, and unstinting, they work, ever aware of the gamble. (Have you the gumption to face your spouse and report, "I guess we'll be losing twenty percent of this year's income, due to those last storms?") Equally, winemakers and vintners are artists. More than harvesting bushels or putting out bottles, they are driven to bring utmost pleasure to your palate.

Of course they will not tell you that. They will more likely nod and say they are just trying to make darn fine wine. That's enough to open the conversation. These are individuals you want to know. In that marvelous conviviality of the winery, you will find yourself fascinated by the final work, and by the artist that created it. So, with these many encounters awaiting, we invite you to go forth with our guide in hand, explore, and savor realms both new and familiar.

—Bart Jackson

OH TASTE AND SEE

A BRIEF GUIDE TO ENJOYING WINE

Much and overmuch has been made about the "correct" way to enjoy wine. Of course, whether you sip or guzzle, swallow or spit, wine is an individual delight. 'Tis your vintage, and the pleasure is all yours. That said, however, experienced oenophiles have found that the art of tasting, like the art of growing, involves a little unhurried time and technique.

Wine embraces all the senses, and it is best to give each one its due. May we suggest the following order:

Sight: Take a moment to behold the beauty of your wine. That all-important first impression, as in so much else, comes from its appearance. Instead of holding it up to a bright light, tilt the wine slightly over something white, like a sheet of paper. Can you read the paper's lettering through the fluid? Examine the color and clarity.

Be it red, white, or pink, look for a fine rim of clear liquid at the edge denoting proper filtering. Are the colors bright and rich, indicating a youthful, aromatic wine? If there are bubbles, do they signify quality with small bubbles forming streams that flow upward, or are they large, individual, and everywhere? As a last step, before you set it down, look at the wine again and briefly consider the vintner's labor appreciatively.

Swirl: Air is wine's greatest enemy and friend. Too much air oxidizes the wine, turning it to vinegar. But expose it to just the right amount, and the wine "breathes," opening up and releasing all its manifold aromas. Swirling gently encourages the flavors of both reds and whites, and it's almost impossible to over swirl. The easiest way is to simply place the glass on a smooth, flat surface. Hold the glass down firmly on the surface by placing your fingers over the base. Now that the glass cannot dart away, spin/swirl it around in tight, smooth circles, making sure the base remains flat on the surface.

The more adventurous may try a second method, in which you hold the glass at the bottom of the stem, keeping it upright, and swirl the wine in a tight, smooth rotation. Remember to keep the glass level. (A little practice with non-staining water saves laundry and embarrassment.)

Good "legs," those lines of drainage on the glass's side viewed after the swirl, are caused by surface tension, and indicate either strong sugar content, or high levels of alcohol.

Smell: Smell is the key to wine's enjoyment. For many folks, wine's greatest joy comes from smelling and deciphering out all those teasing nuances flitting through the bouquet. Even for those less diligent, aroma enriches the experience. No one ever smiled over a glass of wine that smelled like old gym socks. Now, before plunging your nose into the glass, pause a moment. Sniff the wine about an inch or two above the rim. (Be careful, not all wines smell good.)

Then, working toward the bowl, try smelling the wine either in a series of two or three quick sniffs, or one long, gentle inhalation. On this first pass, take note of what you smell. Say the flavors softly to yourself, perhaps. After a moment, try a second scent. Remembering that first smell, what new aromas have you discovered this time?

Wine unleashes layers of aroma. A glass that begins with cherries and light chocolate, may, like some Cabernet Francs, return with an earthy hay-like bouquet later. Technically-oriented tasters may want to study this process more deeply via esters and acids reactions. For the rest of us, simply search and enjoy.

Sip: Sip in a small amount of wine, but don't swallow. About a half ounce is ample for most people to comfortably hold in the mouth while aerating and swishing. Aerating is like a backwards whistle. Suck air through the lips with the wine up against them, without dribbling. (Here again, practicing with a little water over the sink may prove a laundry saver.) Such audible slurping is definitely allowed, encouraged, and draws more flavor-releasing air over the wine.

Now, swish the wine fully over the tongue and mouth and exhale through your nose. Take note of the flavors and feel of your mouth. A tart, harsh feel in the mouth may be caused by excessive acid. Dull flavor and character result from too little acidity, and a bit of a hot burn comes from excessive alcohol. That dry, puckery taste which sticks teeth to gums comes from an absence of sugar, or from heavy tannins (tannic acid) which may have exuded from the grape skins left to darken the wine, or from oak aging. (Thus "tanning" meaning to dry hides.) Remember that your tongue only senses acidity, saltiness, sweetness, and bitterness. All else is actually oratory smells.

Savor: Yes, true ladies do spit wine, and I personally encourage it for maximum enjoyment. First, spitting overflows all the aromas into your mouth. (Recall how smell and air effects wine?) You've just tasted and your mouth is marvelously saturated with wine, which means more surface area. So now, spit out the wine, breathe in deeply, and exhale through your nose. An amazing bouquet of feel, smell, and taste revisits.

Of course, a second reason to opt for spit over swallow if you are sampling several wines is sheer alcohol. It simply may become difficult to judge the wine, let alone hold it steadily.

Finally, pause, reflect, and ask yourself that most important question: Did I enjoy this wine? Wine, after all, is designed for your pleasure. Did the taste linger? Do you want more? If so, mark this one down for a repeat.

Sound: Like smell, sound is a spark of memory. As you hear the wine being uncorked and entering your glass, reflect on the sounds and smells. Then after the taste, recall the many good times these familiar circumstances have brought.

A Brief Note on the Right Glass & Pour

A lot of functionally ideal wine glasses may be found in the dollar store, as well as fine crystal shops. Forget straight sides. For the best taste, look for the teardrop shaped glass. That broad, pear-round bowl atop the stem—the broader the better—allows the wine room to roam in full swirl and release all its finest aromas more completely. Also, the bowl shape also prevents spilage during the swirl.

The tapered rim funnels all those delicious scents directly to your nose well before you begin to sip.

To take fullest advantage of this shape, pour about one ounce (one shot glass full) into the bowl for tasting. When dining, pour about two ounces at a time, then sit back and subject your senses to all the grape's pleasures.

You be the Wine Judge: Comparing Wines in Your Own Blind Taste Test

Is that Cabernet Franc you picked up at a nearby New Jersey winery as good as the expensive-looking bottle your cousin just gave you last Christmas? Obviously the best wine on the planet is the one you like the best. But it can be fun for guests, and enlightening for you, to find out which wines you and your companions actually do prefer, once all the preconceptions, propaganda, and labels are stripped away.

Here are two ways to judge wines:
1. The Blind Test

Organize like a professional tasting. Have an unbiased and very secretive third party decant the wines into plain bottles, or cover them in bulky cloth affixed with tape. (No familiar shapes should appear.) Then number each covered bottle, elect a pourer, and hand out the charts listed below. At evening's end tally up the scores and then uncover the bottles.

The Dionysian Society, *International* **Wine Evaluation Chart**						
Total Scores						
18-20 Extraordinary	Name:			Date:		
15-17 Excellent						
12-14 Good						
9-11 Acceptable	Place:			Theme:	NJ vs Paris	
0-8 Flawed						
Wine	Appearance 2 MAX	Aroma/ BOUQUET 7 MAX	Test/ Texture 5 MAX	Aftertaste 3 MAX	Overall 3 MAX	Total Score 20 MAX

The Dionysian International Wine Evaluation Chart

2. New Jersey Match Contest

The best way to convince reluctant guests that world class competitive wines are produced in Garden State vineyards is to line up six to eight vintages, half New Jersey, half your guests' favorites. Then cut off the foils, cover them in brown paper bags, and tape the bags tightly up. Number the bags in random order and line them up on the table. Ask your guests to match up the bottles with the right wine. Then, for added fun, ask them to list their top three. Use the chart below:

	NJ verses The Judgment of Paris							
	Dionysian Society, *International* **MATCH CHALLENGE**							
	which **WINE is in which BOTTLE**							
	Wine							
Name	New Jersey	New Jersey	New jersey	Far Niente	Silver Oak	Opus One	Pauillac	St Julien
Bart	2	5	4	3	1	7	8	6

The Dionysian International Match Challenge Chart

—Dionysian Charts Courtesy Anthony Fisher,
The Dionysian Society International

Anthony Fisher

Anthony Fisher, esteemed wine expert, educator, and professional judge, began like many of us. At age 21, he and his wife in Elmer, New Jersey began dining out and quickly discovered how much wine enriched the enjoyment of their meals. After a series of home tastings among fellow oenophiles, he joined the American Wine Association where he held the office of Regional Vice President for the five years. He is also a member of the world's oldest wine group—The Dionysian Society, in which he has obtained the Evant—the highest level available in the United States. Turning the hobby into a professional career, Fisher has handled the wine selection and promotion for all Canal Liquors and other stores. Today, wine lovers may seek out Anthony Fisher's advice and choose from his selections at his own store, "The Bottle Barn" in Gibbstown, NJ, (www.bottlebarnwines.com).

NOTES

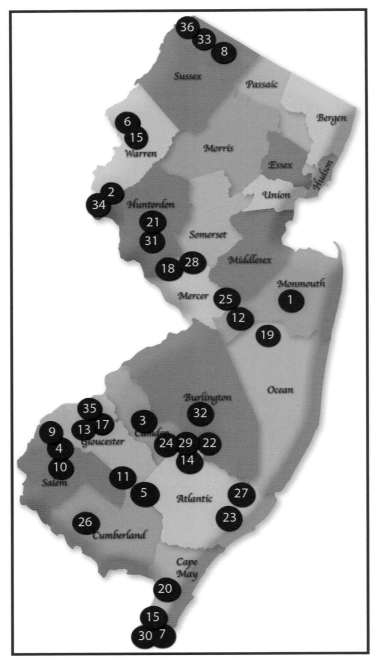

Map of New Jersey's Wineries

New Jersey's Wineries

1. **4 JG's Orchards & Vineyards**
   127 Hillsdale Rd., Colts Neck, NJ 07722
   (908) 930-8066
   www.4jgswinery.com

2. **Alba Vineyard**
   269 Route 627, Milford, NJ 08848
   (908) 995-7800
   www.albavineyard.com

3. **Amalthea Cellars LLC**
   209 Vineyard Rd., Atco, NJ 08004
   (856) 768-8585
   www.amaltheacellars.com

4. **Auburn Road Vineyard LLC**
   119 Sharptown Auburn Rd., Pilesgrove, NJ 08098

   (856) 769-WINE (9463)
   www.auburnroadvineyards.com

5. **Bellview Winery**
   150 Atlantic Street, Landisville, NJ 08326
   (856) 697-7172
   www.bellviewwinery.com

6. **Brook Hollow Winery**
   52 Frog Pond Rd., Columbia, NJ 07832 (908) 496-8200
   www.brookhollowwinery.com

7. **Cape May Winery**
   711 Town Bank Rd., Cape May, NJ 08204
   (609) 884-1169
   www.capemaywinery.com

8. **Cava Winery & Vineyard**
   3629 State Rt. 94, Hamburg, NJ 07419
   (973) 823-9463
   www.cavawinery.com

9. **Cedarvale Winery**
   205 Repaupo Station Rd. Swedesboro, NJ 08085
   (856) 467-3088
   www.cedarvalewinery.com

10. Chestnut Run Farm Winery
66 Stewart Rd., Pilesgrove, NJ 08098
(856) 769-2158
Chestnutrunfarm@aol.com

11. Coda Rossa Winery
1526 Dutch Mill Rd., Franklinville, NJ 08322
(732) 267-0434
www.codarossawinery.com

12. Cream Ridge Winery
145 Route 539, Cream Ridge, NJ 08514
(609) 259-9797
www.creamridgewinery.com

13. DiBella Winery
229 Davidson Rd., Woollwich Twp, NJ 08085
(609) 221-6201
willpto@hotmail.com

14. DiMatteo Vineyards
951 8th Street, Hammonton, NJ 08037
(609) 704-1414
www.dimatteowine@wildblue.net

15. Four Sisters Winery
783 Route 519, Belvidere, NJ 07823
(908) 475-3671
www.foursisterswinery.com

16. Hawk Haven Vineyard & Winery
600 S. Railroad Avenue, Rio Grande, NJ. 08242
(609) 846-7437
www.hawkhavenvineyard.com

17. Heritage Vineyards
480 Mullica Hill Rd., Mullica Hill, NJ 08062
(856) 589-4474
www.heritagestationwine.com

18. Hopewell Valley Vineyards
46 Yard Rd., Pennington, NJ 08534
(866) HVV-WINE (866) 488-9463
www.hopewellvalleyvineyards.com

19. Laurita Winery
35 Archertown Rd., New Egypt, NJ 08533
(800)-LAURITA -528-7482
www.lauritawinery.com

20. Natali Vineyards, LLC
221 N. Route 47, Cape May Court House, NJ 08210
(609) 465-0075
www.natalivineyards.com

21. Old York Cellars
80 Old York Road, Ringoes, NJ 08551
(908-284-9463)
www.oldyorkcellars.com

22. Plagido's Winery
594 N. 1st Rd Hammonton, NJ 08037
(609) 567-4633
www.plagidoswinery.com

23. Renault Winery Inc.
72 N. Bremen Avenue, Egg Harbor City, NJ 08215
(609) 965-2111
www.renaultwinery.com

24. Sharrott Winery
370 S. Egg Harbor Rd., Winslow Township, NJ 08037

(609) 567-WINE (9663)
www.sharrottwinery.com

25. Silver Decoy Winery
610 Windsor Perrineville Rd., Hightstown, NJ 08520
(609) 371-6000
www.silverdecoywinery.com

26. Swansea Vineyards
Shiloh Pike & Randolph Rd., Bridgeton, NJ 08302
(856) 453-5778
www.swanseavineyards.com

27. Sylvin Farms
24 N. Vienna Avenue, Egg Harbor City, NJ 08215
(609) 965-1548
sylvinfarms@comcast.net

28. Terhune Orchards
330 Cold Soil Road, Princeton, NJ 08540
(609-924-2310)
www.terhuneorchards.com

29. Tomasello Winery
225 White Horse Pike, Hammonton, NJ 08037
(800) 666-9463
www.tomasellowinery.com

30. Turdo Vineyards
3911 Bayshore Rd., North Cape May, NJ 08204
(609) 884-5591
www.turdovineyards.com

31. Unionville Vineyards
9 Rocktown Rd., Ringoes, NJ 08551
(908) 788-0400
www.unionvillevineyards.com

32. Valenzano Winery
1090 Route 206, Shamong, NJ 08088 (609) 268-6731
www.valenzanowine.com

33. Ventimiglia Vineyard
101 Layton Rd., Wantage, NJ 07461 (973) 875-4333
www.VentiVines.com

34. Villa Milagro Vineyards
33 Warren Glen Rd., Route 627, Finesville, NJ 08865 (908) 995-2072
www.villamilagrovineyards.com

35. Wagonhouse Winery (@ Grasso Girls Farm Market)
353 Wolfert Station Rd., Mullica Hill, NJ 08062 (609) 780-8019
www.wagonhousewinery.com

36. Westfall Winery
141 Clove R., Montague, NJ 07827 (973) 293-3428
www.westfallwinery.com

Notes

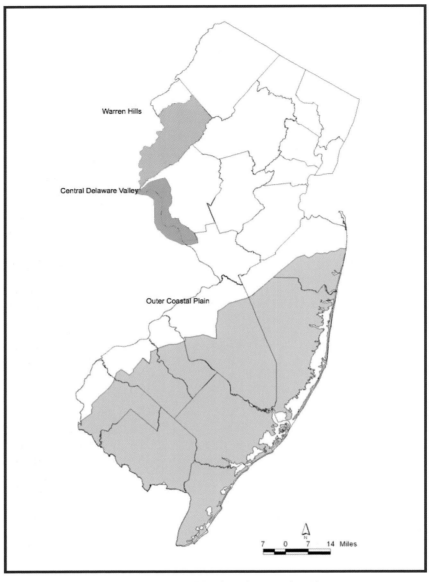

Warren Hills

Central Delaware Valley

Outer Coastal Plain

7   0   7   14 Miles

New Jersey's Viticultural Areas (AVA)

—Courtesy of Dan Ward of Rutgers/NJAES

NEW JERSEY'S VITICULTURAL AREAS

Vines **flourish and thrive in every nook of the Garden State.** Yet because of their recognizably distinctive growing advantages, some sections have been labeled American Viticultural Areas. AVA's are wine growing regions in the United States officially designated by the Alcohol and Tobacco Tax and Trade Bureau. Of the nation's 235, New Jersey embodies three such areas: the Outer Coastal Plain, the Delaware Valley, and the Warren Hills AVA's. Frequently winemakers talk of a wine's appellation, referring to its general place of origin. But to gain approval as a designated Viticultural Area, the vintners must identify and prove unique aspects of the region's physiography that mark it as beneficial to grape farming.

Criteria may include soil type, special drainage, climate, elevation, topography, and historical factors. (In 1919, Prohibition law revenuers stormed through remote, sparsely settled Burlington County, unearthing to their surprise over 100 wineries. Such proud historical nuggets doubtless helped support Outer Coastal Plain vintners' bid for AVA designation.)

The AVA designation typically appears on the wine label just above, or occasionally immediately below the grape name. This indicates that at least 85 percent of that bottle's wine comes from grapes grown within that AVA boundary.

From South to North, New Jersey's AVA's are:

Outer Coastal Plain

This AVA's 2,255,400 acres produce seventy percent of the state's wine and covers New Jersey's flat and piney lower third. It also includes the entire 1.1-million acres of the Pinelands National Reserve. The sandy soil provides excellent drainage, all placed atop a broad, pure, root-accessible aquifer. Gentle sea breezes dry the grapes, and the warm maritime climate allows over two-hundred frost-free days a year.

A broad variety of grapes thrive here:

Merlot, Cabernet Sauvignon, Cabernet Franc and Viognier. Native American grapes such as Cynthiana, Diamond, Ives, and Delaware, have done well here since colonial times, as have later-introduced French Hybrids, Pinot Noir, Chambourcin and Traminette.

Wineries include:
     Amalthea
     Auburn Roads
     Bellview
     Cape May
     Chestnut Run
     Coda Rossa
     DiMatteo
     Hawk Haven
     Heritage Station
     Plagido's
     Natali
     Renault
     Sharrott
     Sylvin Farms
     Swansea, Tomasello
     Turdo
     Valenzano
     Wagonhouse

Central Delaware Valley

These 96,000 acres take in both the Pennsylvania and New Jersey side of the Delaware River, just north of Trenton up to the confluence with the Musconetcong River in the NJ Skylands. The lush, hilly terrain makes it akin in climate and soil to France's Burgundy region. Therefore, conditions are particularly friendly toward French Hybrids, such as Chambourcin, Chancellor, Seyval Blanc, as well as Chardonnay, Riesling, Cabernet Sauvignon, and more recently, Syrah.

Wineries include:
     Cream Ridge
     Hopewell Valley
     Old York Cellars
     Silver Decoy

Warren Hills

These 144,640 acres lie mostly within the borders of Warren County, perched right atop the Central Delaware Valley AVA. From where the Musconetcong flows into the Delaware, the western boundary runs north along the Delaware's banks to just over the Sussex County line. The eastern boundary follows the Musconetcong River for about 10 miles, then cuts sharply north and includes the southernmost Sussex County valley.

In many ways, it is similar to France's Bordeaux region. Although cool, this Appalachian mountainous region's forest-fed, rich soil has proved particularly beneficial to hardy American natives, and imports such as Cayuga, Niagara, Leon Millot, and Seyval Blanc.

Wineries Include:
    Alba
    Brook Hollow
    Four Sisters
    Villa Milagro

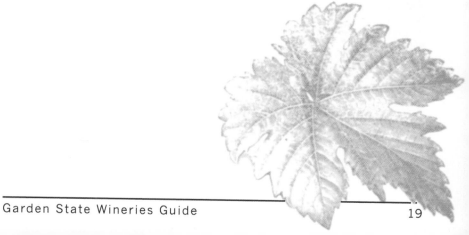

THE YEAR IN WINE

Wine never stops in the Garden State. Following are just a few of the more interesting and unusual events to fill out the wine lover's calendar. Most are set festivals, some simply match the region's seasons. Please note, however, exact dates shift annually. It's best to first check with the individual winery or the Garden State Wine Growers Association to get this year's specifics.

BEGINNING EARLY JANUARY

Bride's Basics: Try to persuade your fiancé to take Dr. Audrey Cross' course. As both winemaker and oft-quoted nutritionist, "Dr. Audrey" will instruct the love of your life how to make meals that are elegant, healthy, and not too difficult to prepare.

Villa Milagro Vineyards (908-955-2072)

JANUARY FRIDAYS: ONWARD

A Classical Happy Hour: Many wineries have happy hours with music, but among the most charming may be found Fridays, 5 to 8 p.m. at Hopewell Valley Winery where Owner Sergio Neri plays operatic favorites on his concert grand Steinway. Music is played weekly, but call to find out when Sergio is hosting.

Hopewell Valley Winery (609-737-4465)

Beginning early February: continued seasonally

Opera Gala: Aficionados of fine music, classic wine, and gourmet foods pack Tomasello Winery's Vintner's Room and feast their full. Tenors and trebles from the Metropolitan and La Scala perform up close and magnificently throughout this four-hour, multi-course, matching-wine extravaganza. Reserve early. Typical schedule is two weekends each:

> **The Winter Gala:** end of January–start of February
> **Totally Tenors Gala:** early and mid-May
> **The Harvest Gala:** early–mid-October
> **Holiday Gala:** early–mid-December
> > **Tomasello Winery (609-666-9463)**

February 14th weekend

Valentines Wine and Chocolate Weekend. Take your beloved to a winery, sample the fine vintages and the array of sumptuous chocolates. Everything she adores stands before her in one room. A young lad hands her a rose. What better way to set a mood.

> **A Garden State Wine Growers Association Event: most wineries participate.**

Early March weekend

Fiesta Benefit for FANA (Foundation for the Assistance of Abandoned Children): Benefitting the orphanage from which two of the owners' grandchildren were adopted, 'tis a celebration plunging visitors into Spanish heritage. Piñatas, music, Spanish cuisine, grape juice tasting for the kids - And ah, the Sangria Wine Release.

> **Cream Ridge Winery (609-259-9797)**

MONTHLY FROM MARCH

Wine Workshop Series: Advanced Sommelier Craig Donofrio offers a selection of sessions, some focusing on a single varietal. Others cover how to conduct a blind tasting, vineyard techniques, overall tasting, and food pairing tips.

Four JG's Vineyards (908-930-8066)

EARLY MAY

Blessing of the Vines: Following the European Medieval tradition, local clergy hold service among the rows of vines and raise prayers for fine weather, sturdy growth, and a bountiful harvest. A very hopeful and joyous festival follows.

Cape May Winery & Vineyard (609-884-1169)
Also check Laurita Vineyard (609-785-8000) for a January Vine Blessing.

MOTHERS DAY IN MAY

Mother's Day Wine Trail Weekend: Wineries outdo each other across the state to make Moms feel at home, many with free wine, fresh flowers, and fun events.
Check Garden State Wine Growers Association (www.newjerseywines.com)

MID-MAY WEEKEND

Cape May World Series of Birding & Wine: Join the globe's most renown (and eccentric) ornithologists as they hustle the state, trying to see who can count the most species in 24 hours. Witness the finish and tally, then drive over to your favorite Cape May Winery where competitors imbibe and boast.

Visit www.birdcapemay.org for dates. Wineries include Cape May, Hawk Haven, Natali, and Turdo vineyards.
This often coincides with The Cape May Wine Festival.

LATE MAY

Hair of the Dog 5k & Pet Expo: For lovers of wine, animals, and fun. Trot the course with about 500+ panting folks, find pet tips and vendors, feast on barbecue, enjoy the array of carnival games, and (after enough wine) take advantage of the K-9 kissing booth. Proceeds benefit the Tri-State Weimaraner Rescue and Res-Q-Pets Animal Rescue.

Silver Decoy Winery (609-371-6000)

Near Memorial Day

Blues & Wine Festival: This annual favorite combines the best of Jersey bands and performers with over two dozen wineries setting forth their latest releases. Take delight in Somerset County's lovely Natirar Estate Park, and pick up some real bargains along with the tasting.

Check Garden State Wine Growers Association (www.newjerseywines.com)

Beginning June

For Ladies Only: Gentlemen are banished from Sharrott's monthly "Ladies Night Out," beginning June, and from Cape May Winery and Vineyard's "Two-Day Ladies Getaway." A blessed and vital separation, perhaps, for both sexes.

Sharrott Winery (609-567-9463)
Cape May Winery (609-884-1169)

July 4th weekend

Independence Day Fireworks Celebration: Pyrotechnics light up the entire Musconetcong River Valley and shakes the ground underneath your picnic spot on the terraced, sloping hillsides of rural Alba Vineyard. Undeniably the best display in the county. Join the jovial crowd.

Alba Vineyard (908-995-7800)

Mid-July

Walk in the Vineyard Winetrail Weekend: For those anxious to observe operations in the field, this is your weekend. Most state wineries have experts standing by to give tours and provide a peek into wine's mystic art.

Check Garden State Wine Growers Association (www.newjerseywines.com)

July–August eves

Celestial Reasoning Nights: Come enjoy the stars under a clear North Jersey sky and the explanations provided by astrophysicist Dr. Ritter, while enjoying her husband Paul's fine wines.

Brook Hollow Winery (908-496-8200)

July–August

Wine Limo Circuit: South Jersey Wine Tours (www.ais-limo.com/winetours) takes you and a few friends merrily tasting in their plush, ultra comfy, chauffeured limousines. A magnificent way to tour safely and in elegant style. "Madam, we have arrived at the winery now. Would you and your friends care to disembark?"

Auburn Road, Cedarvale, and Heritage vineyards.

September Autumns

Leaf Peeping and Wine: The goddess Persephone's Autumnal display shows nowhere more brilliant than in New Jersey's Northwest Skylands. After a day of driving through Stokes Forest or hiking the Appalachian Trail, pause reflectively with a glass of wine from nearby Westfall or Cava Wineries. Also catch Ventimiglia before its September closing.

Cava Winery & Vineyard (973-823-9463)
Ventimiglia Winery (973-875-4333)
Westfall Winery (973-293-3428)

Early September

Jazz It Up Festival: From vintage Dixieland, through Wildwood Days, to current improv, Garden State bands gather amidst the lush, folded hills of Alaire State Park. Barbecue abounds. Statewide wineries offer you a chance to make new discoveries at every booth.

Check Garden State Wine Growers Association (www.newjerseywines.com)

Mid-September–Mid-October

Harvest Festivals: Most wineries hold excellent celebrations of the harvest, and many even let you join in the harvesting. For a full farm experience, try Laurita Winery's Harvest Festival complete with U-pick harvesting of dozens of fruits and vegetables; winery tours; cheese and food seminars; and live music both inside and out. Spend the night at their inn, then saddle up and try the horseback trails.

Meanwhile, Four Sisters Winery celebrates the harvest of its many crops with "Family Fun Days." All age children take hay rides, try the corn maze, pick from the fields and enjoy a day at the farm.

Laurita Winery (609-785-8000)
Four Sisters Winery (908-475-3671)

Typically an October Eve

"Judgment of Paris" Blind Tasting: Come taste the best wines of France, California, and the Garden State. Vote for your favorites, and see who triumphs at the unveiling. (Expect a Jersey victory.)

Amalthea Cellars (856-768-8585)

October 31

Halloween 5k Vampire Sprint: Keep one step ahead of the ghoulies, ghosties, and long-leggedy beasties at this 5k Run and 1-mile Fun Walk beginning 9 a.m. Runners drink free. Awards for toddlers, over 70's—both in and out of costume. $25 registration benefits the Leukemia and Lymphoma Society.

Bellview Winery (856-697-7172)

Late November

Holiday Wine Trail Weekend: Time for the state's wineries to ring in the festive season 'twixt Thanksgiving and New Year. While enjoying their musical parties, check for Sparkling Wine releases, along with each winery's celebration blends.

Check Garden State Wine Growers Association (www.newjerseywines.com)

Yuletide

Christmas & Holiday Dinner: All year round you may take the extensive tasting tour around New Jersey's oldest winery, then follow it up with a five-to-seven course, wine-paired gourmet dinner. But for the December holidays, when the field fowl and game are in season, Executive Chef Joseph Degennero presents a feast worthy of your family's celebration.

Renault Winery (609-965-2111)

GARDEN STATE WINERY PROFILES

THE 4 JG'S VINEYARDS

127 Hillsdale Road, Colts Neck, NJ 07722
(908-930-8066)
www.4jgswinery.com

Owner: John Sr., Janet, John Jr. and Jill Giunco
Winemakers: Janet G. and Craig Donofrio

Public hours: September–October: weekends, 1–5ᴾᴹ; remaining weekends, frequent special events **($5 affords complete tastings, vineyard tour, and souvenir glass.)**

Events: Monthly Colts Neck Wine workshop series ($30 ea.); Valentines Day Celebration. Thanksgiving Festival. Vineyard Walk.

Description: The ten wines produced by the four Giuncos reflect a fine blend of time-proven farming techniques, and current scientific technology. The generations of Giuncos who have tilled Monmouth County's dark, fertile soils since 1801 passed to John Sr. a treasury of wisdom. Almost instinctively he knows the right canopy management that promotes aeration and demands minimal spraying. His wife Janet, the primary winemaker, employs the advice and testing methods of such expert friends as Napa's Peter Mondavi.

When the Giuncos expressed a desire to return to the family trade and launch a wine farm, John's mother warned them, "Be careful what you wish for." But children seldom listen. By 1999, they purchased the farm. As planting began, Janet left her IBM job, and John cut his involvement in his land development company.

Son John and daughter Jill (the final 2 Gs) helped plant the remaining 28 acres in a verdant oasis of tranquility, surrounding the 1725 farmhouse and barn.

Today the Four JGs have developed as large and loyal following of weekend visitors. In a homecoming atmosphere, old faces and new enjoy 4JG's unique sangria (based on a different wine each time,) light-sipping Cayuga, or their flagship Chambourcin Riserva '05. Everyone wants to pitch in. You might even find yourself pulling leaves with 4JG's renowned and intriguing neighbors who help when in town.

If you like the tastings and vineyard walks, don't miss 4JG's Colt's Neck Wine Workshop. Advanced Sommelier Craig Donofrio focuses each session on a single varietal, explaining regional differences, vineyard techniques, tasting and food pairing tips. Sample, learn, and take delight.

Owner's Most Prized & Favored Wines:
Chambourcin Riserva 2005, $15.99
Cayuga White 2007, $10.99
Cabernet Franc 2007, $16.99
Vignole 2008, $21.99
(Plus six other blends and blushes)

Awards include: 2008 New Jersey Wine Growers Association Best Hybrid of the Year; Best Estate Grown—LA World of International Wines Festival & San Francisco Chronicle Silver & Bronze.

Harvest season: Varieties are harvested early September through early November.

Vineyard production: Thirty-three-acres containing Chardonnay, Cabernet Franc, Cayuga, Chambourcin, and Chancellor varieties. All wines come strictly from JG's estate grapes.

Facility: Cozy tasting room and private side room in the 1725 estate house are, weather permitting, typically bypassed in favor of a sprawling outside tented and tabled venue, beneath the huge and shady trees.

Directions: From Center Freehold, or Route 18 Exit 25, get onto Route 79 North Proceed up to Vanderburg Road—take it right. After 1.4 miles, Vanderburg crosses Boundary Road and becomes Crine Rd. Go .4 miles, turn left onto Hillsdale Road, proceed .6 miles. "4 J.G.'s" sign and driveway are on right.

Part of the Central Wine Trail, including Laurita, Cream Ridge, and Silver Decoy vineyards.

ALBA VINEYARD

269 Route 627, Village of Finesville, Milford, NJ 08848
908-995-7800, wines@albavineyard.com
www.albavineyard.com

Owner: Tom Sharko
Winemaker: John Altmaier

Public hours: *All year:* Sunday–Friday, 11^{AM}–5^{PM}; Saturday, 11^{AM}– 6^{PM}. **($10 affords complete tastings and souvenir glass.)**

Events: Scheduled tours daily during public hours. July Fireworks Celebration; Monthly Music Under the Arbor; Several music & picnic weekends; Wine 101 instruction.

Description: The fertile silt loam atop the slanting limestone base and the near-maniacal attention to each vine and step of the processing. Such are the ingredients that have made famous the wines from France's Burgundy and Bordeaux regions. And such are the ingredients feeding the equally fine vintages of Alba Vineyard, in the Warren Hills Viniculture area.

Perched on the sharp flank of the Musconetcong and Delaware River valleys, Alba's forty-two rolling acres of carefully patch-worked varietals bask in day long sun, as picnicking visitors delight in the three-hundred-degree vistas of forested ridges. Ideally, visit during July Fireworks Day. After tasting and browsing the

Musconetcong Museum in the 190-year-old barn, spread your blanket among the hillside vines, and await the county's foremost thunderous display.

For owner Tom Sharko, Alba was a fluke turned into a calling. In 1997, as a thriving high-craft woodworker, Sharko eyed the failed winery and its old barns with thoughts of expanding his wood shop. Somehow, the potential for a fresh winery took hold, and Sharko transferred his lifelong precision and detailed focus from fine woods to fine wines. Experimentation led to only French oak for aging. Alba also employs a tight pack of 2,400, rather than the typical six-hundred to eight-hundred vines per acre; a method pushing more fruit, and less vine growth. Recently, impressed by these techniques, Argentinean vintners invited Sharko to help renovate their newly exporting vineyards. But the real proof of north Jersey's ability to compete internationally lies in your own palate, and taking the short road to Alba's tasting rooms.

Owner's most prized & favored wines:
Pinot Noir 2004, $24.99
Dry Riesling 2005, $13.99
Chardonnay Barrel Reserve 2004, $14.99
(Check for current vintages. Alba also has sixteen others including a Port and Sparkling Brut.)

Awards include: 2009 Winery of the Year in NJ Wine Competition; 4 times Garden State Winery of the Year; 2009 World Wine Championship: 4 Silver medals, 1 Best Buy, and 1 Platinum; a host of medals from competitions ranging from Pacific Rim, Los Angeles, Dallas, to the International Eastern and Finger Lakes competitions.

Harvest season: Varieties are harvested mid-September through early November.

Vineyard production: Forty-two acres containing eighteen varieties and producing eleven-thousand cases annually. Some grapes purchased from other Garden State vineyards.

Facility: Benches and picnic spots throughout terraced vineyards. Full tasting room in their 1801 old stone farm building. Tents available for outdoor weddings and festivals.

Directions: *From the south,* take Route 29 North until it ends in Frenchtown; turn left then quick right onto Harrison Street and follow it into Milford. Go straight at the light onto Route 519 North, and continue 10 minutes to a stop sign. Bear left at stop sign onto Route 627. Go 2 miles, Alba is on right.

From Route 78, Take I-78 to exit 7 (Bloomsbury). Bear right off ramp onto Route 173 West). After 1.3 miles, bear left onto Route 639 West, towards Riegelsville. Go 2.8 miles, bear right onto Route 519 South, which becomes Route 627 South. Go two miles, Alba is on the right.

Part of the Warren County Wine Trail, including Alba, Brook Hollow, Four Sisters, and Villa Milagro Vineyards.

AMALTHEA CELLARS

209 Vineyard Road, Atco, NJ 08004
856-768-8585, winery@amaltheacellars.com
www.amaltheacellars.com

Owner & Winemaker: Louis Caracciolo

Public hours: *All year:* Saturday and Sunday, 11ᴬᴹ–5ᴾᴹ. **(Free tastings.)**

Events: Informal, free tours daily during public hours. Several tasting festivals, held throughout the year. Gourmet dinners held at adjacent Green Dragon Tavern.

Description: Louis Caracciolo is a passionate competitor, and those who visit Amalthea Cellars are the beneficiaries. Employing a blend of today's technologies and Medieval traditions, Louis produces vintages that have twice, in blind taste tests, triumphed handsomely over the best (and most expensive) wines of California and France. Amalthea stands as one of several vineyards proving that world-class fine wine does indeed come from the Garden State.

You will first want to take entrance into the intimate vault of Amalthea's tasting room, and breathe the atmosphere of this wine sanctuary. Under the pourer's tutelage, discern the delicate differences between the Europa II through VII–each blending precise amounts of Cabernet Sauvignon, Cabernet Franc, and Merlot. Before you rush to buy, compare fully the Cellars' four Chardonnays, or her three Cabernet Sauvignons. Oak, age, and vintner's craft tease out the individual tastes.

Then, with a full glass of your favorite, sit beneath the tall pitch pines of the Barrens. Here, in 1976, amid the sun, breeze, and fast-draining sugar sand of this Outer Coastal Plain, Carracciolo first panted Chancellor grapes and launched Amalthea. A hearty blend of his grandfather Emilio's traditional touch, and the scientific, Old World techniques, learned at Pratt Institute, plus hands-on experience in Bordeaux, France, all merged to form this vintner's original artistry.

Doubtless the best way to experience Amalthea's well-aged vintages is to step next door and dine in the 125-year-old Green Dragon Tavern. The food, oft prepared by Marie (Louis' 84-year-old Mom), in every way matches the labors of her son.

Owner's most prized & favored wines:

Europa Series (Cabernet Sauvignon, Cabernet Franc, Merlot blends), from $20.99 to $27.99

Cabernet Sauvignon Clone II 2007, $16.99

Merlot Reserve 2006, $19.99; 2005–$38.99; 2004, $74.99

Chardonnay Reserve 2006, $18.99

Syrah 2007, $15.99

(Plus nineteen other offerings including the 2007 Sarah, Chancellor Reserve, Rkatsiteli Cask 27, and semi-dry's Villard and Calisto Rouge.)

Awards include: A long list of State, Regional, and International awards.

Harvest season: Varieties are harvested mid-September through early November.

Vineyard production: Eleven acres containing Cabernet Franc, Cabernet Sauvignon, Chancellor, Chardonnay, Merlot, Riesling, Rkatsiteli, Viognier varieties. These produce three-thousand cases annually. Up to fifty percent of grapes contracted, under owner's supervision, from other Garden State vineyards.

Facility: Within the winery, the cloistered tasting room and expansive gift shops have a feel of traditional comfort. These open out onto porch and tree shaded seating areas outside, overlooking the vines. Across the lawn stands Green Dragon Inn with long diner tables, private rooms, and double doors opening onto tents outside.

Directions: *From the NJ Turnpike,* take Exit 4 onto Route 73 South. Proceed several miles through Berlin then take Route 30 East two miles. Look for winery sign at third traffic light, and turn right onto Vineyard Road. Winery is one mile down.

This Route also works from Route I-295, Exit 36.

The Atlantic City Expressway, Exit 31 also leads to Route 73 North, which leads you up to Route 30 East, proceed as above.

From the south, Take Route 54 to Route 30 West, or from the north, take Route 206 to Route 30 West. Either way, proceed to Center Avenue, take it left, turn right on Fifth Avenue, left on Washington Avenue and quickly right onto Vineyard Road. Winery is a few hundred yards up on the left.

Part of the common northern Outer Coastal Plain Wine Trail, including Amalthea, Plagido, Sharrott, and Valenzano vineyards.

AUBURN ROAD VINEYARD & WINERY

117 Sharptown-Auburn Road, Pilesgrove, NJ 08098
856-769-9463, info@auburnroadvineyards.com
www.auburnroadvineyards.com

Owner: Dave Davis & Shannon Kilpatrick, Scott & Julianne Donnini
Winemaker: Julianne Donnini

Public hours: *All year:* Friday, 4ᴾᴹ–8ᴾᴹ; Saturday, 12ᴾᴹ–8ᴾᴹ; Sunday, 12ᴾᴹ–5ᴾᴹ, Or call for appointment. **(Free tastings.)**

Events: Hourly, free vineyard tours all weekend long or by appointment. Also check out "Local Live Music Saturdays" and "What's for Dinner Fridays."

Description: Cut away from suburbia's edge, along Auburn Road's broad South Jersey horizons, and follow the winery sign back into a touch of the Continent. The sign "Enoteca" (Italian for "Wine Repository") leads you into a surprisingly large, warm, quietly festive tasting room. More than a name, Enoteca embraces the atmosphere of a leisurely European cafe, where one searches that ideal Auburn blend, while local musicians in the corner fill the room with their own compositions. It is an oasis for hours, not moments.

Blends are an Auburn signature, designed by Julianne Donnini, one of the state's few female winemakers, thus far. The aptly gold-awarded Classico 2007, blends four varietals into a Super Tuscan with robust body. The 2007 Rustica also provides the full flavor of its Cabernet Franc and Merlot elements.

Auburn Road came into being as a four-way abrupt career shift. Finance and law are fine occupations, but sometimes you seek more tangible fruits of your labors. At least so was the plan of J.P. Morgan financial comptroller Dan Kilpatrick, his wife, project manager Shannon, and lawyer couple, Julianne and Scott Donnini. "I didn't want to cut a lawn," so we took my Dad's inheritance, and invested in a dream–launched a pilot winery" says Dave. A year after the 2003 purchase, they planted their first two-acre test winery on enriched farmland that initially nurtured hay, soy and pasturage.

Now, in five short years, the still-working team has tripled that acreage. Join this thriving investment in a dream for "What's for Dinner Friday" evenings or "Local Live Music" Saturdays.

Owner's most prized & favored wines:

Classico, $18.99
Good Karma 2007, $14.99
Sole 2008, $15.99
Pinot Grigio 2009, $16.99

(Plus five other varieties, including several blends from their estate grown Cabernet Sauvignon, Merlot, San Genovese, Pinot Grigio and Chambourcin.)

Awards include: 2008 New Jersey Wine Competition Golds: Pinot Grigio 2007, Classico 2007; Silvers: Merlot Reserve 2007, Chardonnay, Chardonnay reserve; Bronzes: Rustica, Vidal Blanc, Rosalita Blush. 2009 NJ Competition, eight medals. Finger Lakes Competition Sliver: Classico.

Harvest season: From early September, through third week in October.

Vineyard production: Six acres containing five varieties and producing two-thousand cases annually. Up to fifty percent of grapes are purchased from other Garden State vineyards.

Facility: Inviting tasting room, ample for dinners, conferences, and small weddings. The outside patio and shaded lawns, with tents available, overlook the vineyard.

Directions: Using Jersey Turnpike Exit 2, or your favorite method, get to Route I-295 South, and get off at Exit 4 (Woodstown). Merge left onto Route 48. Follow it until it ends, turning left onto Route 40 East. Pass Cowtown Rodeo on your right, then take your first left onto Sharptown-Auburn Road. Winery is one mile ahead on your left.

Part of a common weekend Wine Trail including Swansea, Auburn Road, Heritage, and Cedarvale vineyards.

BELLVIEW WINERY

150 Atlantic Street Landisville, NJ 08326
856-697-7172, jim@bellviewwineries.com
www.bellviewwinery.com

Owner: Jim & Nancy Quarella; aided by sons Lee, Scott & Tony
Winemaker: Jim Quarella

Public hours: *All year:* every day, 11ᴬᴹ–5ᴾᴹ; Closed some days in January. **(Free complete tastings.)**

Events: Saturday, 2ᴾᴹ vineyard/winery tours ($10, includes souvenir glass.); Periodic Cooking Demonstrations; Intro to Wine Tasting courses; Halloween 5k Vampire Sprint; October Italian Festival; August Jazz Festival; and Seafood Festival and Classic Car Show.

Description: If the grape grows well in the Garden State, odds are you can find it well grown on the Quarella family winery. From the hearty North American Ives to the smooth Germanic Lemberger, twenty varieties span its thirty-acre Outer Coastal vineyard. Here is an ideal place to sip and discover. Those a bit boggled at the selection may want to register for Belview's excellent Intro to Wine Tasting course.

In 1914, Italian émigré Angelo Quarella purchased and named this Pine Barrens' farm Bellview. Five generations later, great-grandson Jim Quarella, wife Nancy, and his sons still maintain the family farm, now expanded to 150 acres of fruit trees and vegetables. Turning a hobby into a cash crop, they cleared the additional vineyard acres and planted in 2000.

It has been this generational farmer's wisdom that allowed the Quarella's to attempt such an ambitious varietal array. Scientific study and schedules for leaf pulling, spraying, harvesting, etc. are all tweaked by that instinctual feel for each grape type and condition. Witness the subtleties in their full, red Petit Verdot or the dry, smooth Viognier.

Machine aficionados will want to come at harvest time to witness the giant mechanical grape harvester in action. More celebratory visitors will attend the October Italian festival with food, music, and bocci on the expansive lawn; or the August Seafood Festival with local catches and live jazz. Of course, you can always plan your party in the welcoming Courtyard Room to coincide with the July Dandelion Wine Release.

Owner's most prized & favored wines:
Syrah, $14.99
Cabernet Franc, $18.99
Viognier, $18.99
Lemberger, $17.99
(Plus twenty-eight other offerings coming from their vineyard's Ives, Traminette, Fredonia, Muscat Ottonel, Sangiovese, Touriga Nacionale, Petit Verdot, Tinta Cao, and many other varietals.)

Awards include: Crystillina 2007 won the Governor's Cup and the silver at Finger Lakes International Wine Competition. 2008 Best Dessert Wine in New Jersey.

Harvest season: Labor Day through mid-October.

Vineyard production: Thirty-five acres planted; containing twenty grape varieties, producing one-hundred tons of grapes and 6250 cases annually. All the grapes are grown on their estate. Twenty-five percent of their fruit is sold to other wineries.

Facility: A large full tasting room and the separate Courtyard room each hold parties of up to fifty. Wide-tented lawns and picnic facilities outside host larger parties, and even boast a Bocci court. Also, Bellview has a WiFi Network Setup—so grab the laptop and come on over.

Directions: *From Central Jersey,* find your way onto Route 206 South, until it enters Hammonton and becomes Route 54 South. Follow Route 54, turn right onto Route 40 West, and proceed 1.7 miles. Make right onto Central Avenue. Go .3 miles, turn right onto Atlantic Street and proceed to the winery .3 miles on left.
From Route 295, follow Route I-295 South until it becomes Route 42. Take Route 42 South to Route 55 South, exiting on 39A for Route 40. Take Route 40 East to Route 690 (Weymouth Road) and turn sharply left onto Central Ave. .3 miles leads you to a right onto Atlantic Street. The winery is .3 miles on your left.

Part of a popular weekend Wine Trail, around the Hammonton Area, including Amalthea , DiMatteo, Plagido, Sharott, and Tomasello vineyards.

BROOK HOLLOW WINERY

52 Frog Pond Road, Colombia, NJ 07832
908-496-8200, winemaker@brookhollowwinery.com
www.brookhollowwinery.com

Owner and Winemaker: Paul Ritter

Public hours: *All year:* Saturday and Sunday, 12ᴾᴹ–5ᴾᴹ. **($3 buys a complete tasting and a souvenir glass.)**

Events: Tour both the vineyard and this working farm on weekends. In season, pick your own pumpkins and apples. October brings the Pig Roast. Summer nights, a periodic Wine Under the Stars affords an opportunity to sip a vintage and learn the constellations. Also, wagon rides for all ages.

Description: Sumptuous wine is just part of the experience that draws visitors far north to the red barns on rural Frog Pond Road. Behind the eight acres of vines, first planted in 2002, spreads the 175-acre Brook Hollow farm whose fields offer children a chance to pick their own pumpkins, raspberries, and all fruits in season. Those not plucked by guests, are harvested for Brook Hollow's Spiced Apple, Blueberry, Cherry, Cranberry, Peach, and Strawberry wines. It's a fruit wine lovers' magnet, and many of the selections sell out early.

But tasters should not ignore this vineyard's impressive table wines. State biologist Paul Ritter has been making wine since his teens, helping his grandfather with the family hobby. All his scientific, agricultural, and early enology skills have given him a fine sense of getting the most out of grapes. Even Brook Hollow's deep folded valley benefits the vines, assuring a late frost.

On your way back through the barn to the taste the enchantingly popular Sauvignon Blanc, the seldom found semisweet Gewurztraminer white, or Chambourcin hinting of chocolate and cherry, pause a bit. Browse among the intriguing collection of old, hand farm implements and household tools that the great-grandfolks once wielded, when life was more of a sweat.

Explore Brook Hollow's winery and working farm any weekend, but don't miss the October Pig Roast. And what could be more romantic than a starry night, a glass of full-bodied Brook Hollow Red, and astrophysicist Gary Swangin on the next blanket to explain all the celestial wonderment before you?

Owner's most prized & favored wines:

Proprietor's Red, $15.99
Chambourcin, $14.99
Cabernet Sauvignon Reserve 2004, (Sold out—look for next vintage.)
Sauvignon Blanc, $12.99

(Plus 15 other offerings including a Holiday Red, Gewurztraminer, and both a dry and semisweet Strawberry.)

Harvest season: Varieties are harvested mid-September through mid-October.

Vineyard production: Eight acres in grapes containing such varieties as Niagara, Cayuga, Vidal, Leon Millot, Farouche and Chambourcin are harvested, and produce about 1050 cases annually. All of the grapes used grow on the estate.

Facility: An intriguing museum of farm tools, memorabilia, and farm-fresh fruits for sale fills the front of the converted barn which leads to the tasting room in back. The two-hundred-seating tent or the abundant picnic facilities on the broad lawns take things outdoors.

Directions: *By your favorite method,* get onto I-80. Take Exit 4A as you approach the Delaware River, and proceed north on Route 94. Proceed approx. four miles to Frog Pond Road. The winery is a short way on your right.

Part of the Warren Wine Trail, including Alba, Brook Hollow, Four Sisters, and Villa Milagro Vineyards.

CAPE MAY WINERY & VINEYARD

711 Townbank Road, Cape May, NJ 08204
609-884-1169
www.capemaywinery.com

Owner: Arthur Craig
Winemaker: Darren Hesington

Public hours: July–April: daily, 12ᴾᴹ–6ᴾᴹ; January–December: daily, 12ᴾᴹ–5ᴾᴹ.
(Tasting of two wines is free; $5 affords complete tastings and souvenir glass.)

Events: Scheduled tours, usually 3ᴾᴹ, are held daily during public hours **($20.)**;
Self-guided are free. Myriad others include: Early May Blessing of the Vines;
Champagne Sundays **($3.)**; October Grand Harvest Festival; Picnic box lunches;
Girlfriends two-day Getaway; Case Club; and CCB Futures Tasting.

Description: "All good food is enhanced by the right wine," states owner Arthur
Craig. Thus, guests sipping their way through Cape May's ample tasting room
and gift shop have the chance to browse volumes of wine-oriented recipes. Craig
comes by his food/wine partnering proclivity through long experience. In 1978,
he and his family founded Cape May's Washington Inn where he spent decades
trying to embellish the experience of fine dining. This led naturally to his interest
in select wines.

In 1820, coffin maker Isaac Smith owned and operated on the vineyard's current site. Choosing these fertile soils, Craig bought the Isaac Smith estate in 1980, planted in 1990, and by 1994 his Winery and Vineyard began delighting Cape May tourists. Turning his full attention to wine, Arthur entrusted owner-ship of the Washington Inn to son Michael and the Lucky Bones Backwater Grille to son David.

Yet this scarcely ended his love of partnering food and wine. Craig's team began structuring wines to specifically compliment certain dishes. Beginning with Isaac Smith Fini Blanc for cheeses and hors d'oeuvres, then moving to the Barrel Fermented Chardonnay and Cape May Merlot for entrees, and finishing with the Isaac Smith Port for desserts, Cape May Vineyards employs the Outer Coastal Plain's ideal wine climate to complete the ideal feast. The expanded Cape May Winery's Victorian-style building affords settings of simple elegance in a fine dining atmosphere and allows you to test Mr. Craig's maxim about food and wine. Come bring your own picnic, or enjoy any of the catered meals and events.

Owner's most prized & favored wines:
Cabernet Sauvignon 2007, $20
Barrel Fermented Chardonnay 2007, $18
Syrah 2008, $18
Isaac Smith Cabernet Sauvignon 2006, $20, (almost out—look for next vintage.)
(Plus seventeen others including varietals, blends, reds, whites, a blush and a port. New reserves are on the way.)

Awards include: 2008 Wine Growers Association Gold: '06 Barrel fermented Chardonnay, Silver: '07 Cape May Chardonnay and Cape May Red, Isaac Smith Port; Bronze: Cabernet Franc, Pinot Grigio, Merlot, Victorian White, Riesling.

Harvest season: Varieties are harvested mid-September through early November.

Vineyard production: Nine and one-half acres containing ten varieties and producing almost 9,000 cases annually. Another fifteen acres currently grow new vines. Up to thirty percent of grapes purchased from other Garden State vineyards. (These comprise the Isaac Smith Coffin labels.)

Facility: Spacious tasting room and gift shop; upstairs rooms and large, vine-covered picnic deck; Victorian-style Barrel Room set for private tastings of up to forty. Food and dining are available. Outdoor tent and sprawling lawn provide for large parties.

Directions: *Take the Garden State Parkway South* to mile marker 0, bear right onto Route 109 North, follow it onto Route 9 South and take the jughandle at Seashore Road, making a right. Make a left at Townbank. #711 is 1/2 mile down on right.
From Cape May Ferry: Drive straight out of the ferry lot, turning left onto Seashore Road at 4th light. #711 is 1/2 mile down on right.

Part of the Cape May Wine Trail, including Cape May, Turdo, and Natali Vineyards.

CAVA WINERY & VINEYARD

3619 Route 94, Hamburg, NJ 07419
973-823-9463, info@cavawinery.com
www.cavawinery.com

Owners: Anthony Riccio & wife Deneah Bledsoe
Winemakers: Anthony Riccio (the art), Deneah Bledsoe (the science)

Public hours: March–December: Saturdays, 1^{PM}–6^{PM}; many Saturday morns find Cava at Crystal Springs Farm Market. **($5 affords four tastings and $10 offers limitless tastings.)**

Events: Cava is partnered with nearby Mountain Creek Resort in Vernon for a twenty percent discount and mutual events. Seasonal food pairing dinners; Wine instruction seminars.

Description: Pressed against the eastern flank of the Sussex Appalachians, the grand arching Cava Winery and adjacent Victorian train station evoke memories of 19th Century gentility getaways. These forested ridges once seemed reserved for the wealthy citified few, with cash disposable. But now, Cava's environs embrace hikers, golfers, autumnal leaf lovers, and cyclists. And all may find day's-end renewal at this piedmont vineyard—perhaps with a glass of bold, warming D'Oro Red.

Beneath the winery's sturdy oaken beams, owners Anthony and Deneah Riccio have drenched their tasting room with atmosphere Italiane. Chianti-red tablecloths, the warmly paneled walls laden with intriguing art, all reflect the Mediterranean feel of Cava's wines. Her popular Ferro Red offers an intense savor, with a touch of cherry. Whether sampling one of Cava's reds, or even her light, fruity Magnesio, visitors often remark on the tangy touch of tannin seeping through from these Skylands' mountain soils.

In such a setting, young Anthony labored as a field hand and developed his first taste of farming satisfaction. His shift from the realm of business to more spiritual viniculture came when, as he puts it, "I dreamt I was in some sort of commercial nightmare, and I awoke to find it was real." Employing his study, heritage, and wife Deneah's scientific training, the Riccio's planted five acres in 2005, emulating a Californian method of variably spaced rows, and adapting regionally optimum fruit.

The winery doors opened in 2008, bearing the name Cava, reflecting the colonial mine caves which pepper these mineral-rich hills. Come enjoy the mountain's new riches.

Owner's most prized & favored wines:
D'Oro Red, $23
Cava Ferro, $23
Magnesio, $13
Zincato, $13

(Plus twelve other offerings including an interesting Sangiovese Cabernet blend, a Riccio Misto TreFratelli blend, and a sweeter Zinfandel and Riccio Blush.)

Awards include: 2009 S.F. Chronicle Wine Competition Bronze: Magnesio, Cava Ferro; 2009 International. Eastern Wine Competition Bronze: D'Oro Red.

Harvest season: Varieties are harvested mid-September through mid-October.

Vineyard production: Five acres of vines, containing Cabernet Franc, Norette, Traminette varieties and producing three-hundred cases annually. Up to twenty-five percent of grapes purchased from other Garden, and Empire State vineyards.

Facility: The wide tasting room comfortable seats sixty diners. The entire building holds full dining service, a 25 x 25 foot dance floor, with all the electronic facili-ties. Guests may also overflow into the outdoor patio which faces the vineyard and mountains above.

Directions: *From the NJ Turnpike North,* exit onto Interstate I-287 North and proceed up to Route 23 Northwest. Follow 23 into Hamburg, and turn right onto Route 94 North ((Vernon Avenue.) The winery is .8 miles on left.

From Route 80, take exit 34 onto Route 15 North. Follow Route 15 to Route 94 North (N. Church Road) and proceed as above.

Part of the Sussex County Wine Trail, including Cava, Ventimiglia, and Westfall vineyards.

CEDARVALE WINERY & VINEYARD

205 Repaupo Station Road, Logan Township, NJ 08085
856-467-3088, info@cedarvalewinery.com
www.cedarvalewinery.com

Owner: Ed & Marsha Gaventa
Winemaker: Ed Gaventa

Public hours: *All year:* Thursday & Friday, 12^{PM} to 7^{PM}; Saturday, 11^{AM} to 7^{PM}; Sunday 11^{AM} to 5^{PM}; or by appointment. **($5 affords complete tastings and souvenir glass.)**

Events: Music Night held Fridays monthly. Halloween Costume Party. Special Party Nights on weekends; buy a bottle or glass and meet new friends. Try the South Jersey Wine Trail Limo to visit this winery in appropriate luxury.

Description: Fruit wine lovers have found a haven. All the blueberries, strawberries, peaches, and even nectarines found in Cedarvale bottles, come straight from the two-hundred-acre Gaventa family farm surrounding the vineyard. Their subtlety and fullness of fruit comes through, just as the grapes forming Cedarvale's uniquely smooth Merlot and light-oaked Chardonnay.

Entering the tasting room, visitors can almost sense the promise of this young winery. The walls, which only went up a year ago, bear such enthusiasms as

---

　　　　　　　　Garden State Wineries Guide

"Wine is bottled poetry" and Galileo's claim that "Wine is sunlight, held together by water." With the first 2007 vintage, Cedarvale began garnering awards. After having effervescent owner Marcia Gaventa pour you a Pinot Grigio or Merlot, you might just ask husband-and- winemaker Ed Gaventa for a barrel sample of things to come. Then you too may appreciate Cedarvale's aura of anticipation.

Wine may be sunshine and poetry, but to those ingredients Ed has added a lot of sweat and four generations of farming instinct. Ask about his leaf-pulling rotation system. Originally asked to produce grapes for other area wineries, in 2004 the Gaventa's decided to grow and process for themselves. Resisting the title of "Marcia's Vineyard," they opted for the farm's former Trade-As name, more reflective of the bordering cedar swamps.

Still managing the fruit farm, Gaventa seeks to expand his five acres of five varietals. Watch for Saval Blanc, Traminette, and Chambourcin in the future. Fans of Pine Barrens culture should visit on Monday eves when local musicians present their newest creations.

Owner's most prized & favored wines:
Pinot Grigio, $16.99
Chardonnay, $16.99
Merlot, $18.00
Nectarine, $14.99
(Plus four other offerings including fruit wines of Blueberry, Cherry, and Peach.)

Awards include: 2009 NJ Wine Growers Association Silver: 2007 Merlot.

Harvest season: Varieties are harvested mid-September through mid-October.

Vineyard production: Five acres containing Cabernet Franc, Chardonnay, Merlot, Pinot Grigio, Syrah varieties. These plus the estate-grown fruits produce six-hundred cases of wine annually.

Facility: Three cold storage rooms aid in wine processing. The inviting tasting room serves mid-size crowds for music and fun. A small party tent can be erected for outdoor parties.

Directions: By your favorite method, get onto Route I-295/130. Take Exit 14 (just south of Paulsboro and north of Route 322) onto Repaupo Station Road, and proceed northwest .4 mile to the winery on your left.

Part of the South Jersey Wine Tours allowing you to take the limo and arrive in style at the Auburn Road, Cedarvale, Heritage, and Wagonhouse vineyards.

CHESTNUT RUN FARM WINERY

66 Stewart Road, Pilesgrove, NJ 08098
856-769-2158, Chestnutrunfarm@aol.com

Owners: Bob & Lise Clark
Winemaker: Bob Clark

Public hours: Winery is not open for public visiting.

Description: Not all fine wine comes from grapes alone. At your next Garden State Winegrowers' festival, stop by Bob and Lise Clark's tent and let them convince you what delicately blended exotic pears and apples can do. The sweat and magic takes place back at their twenty-two-acre farm where they first planted their trees in 1986.

Advancing up the hand-smoothed gravel drive, past the sheep, by the vegetable plots, and the espalier (two-dimensionally-grown) Fuji apples, the sense of independence becomes plain. And crowning them all stands the pears. The Clarks, a pair of biomedical Ph.D.'s, opted out of academia and business to create life on their own terms. Prior to NAFTA and online competition, their Chestnut Run had carved out a thriving niche as a supplier of fancy fruits and vegetables. Then, six years ago, as markets dried up, Clark saw an equally profitable use for his orchards. Ever flexible to reality, this agricultural entrepreneur set his fruits to the press.

Today, he calls himself simply a farmer who sells his fruit as wine. Yet the results are anything but simple. Using Hosui, Yoi Nashi, Shinko, and five other exotic pear varieties, he ferments each separately then blends his unique and subtle pear wines. Both the pear and Fuji apple vintages have become remarkably popular at Asian BYOB restaurants. (Try the Spiced Pear with Thai dishes.)

Alas, the Clarks' unlicensed farm allows for neither sampling nor selling. But check out all Winegrowers' Association festivals and local farmers markets. Then lay down a stock and experiment at pairing it with your favorite banquet plates.

Owner's most prized & favored wines:

Spiced Sweet Asian Pear Wine, $11.50
Dry Pear Wine, $11.50
Semi Sweet Pear Wine, $11.50
Fuji Apple Wine (all apple, unblended), $11.50

Awards include: New Jersey Wine Growers Association Silver: Semi Sweet Pear 2008; Bronze: Dry Pear, Spiced Sweet Asian Pear, and Fuji Apple: both 2007 and 2008.

Harvest season: Varieties are harvested late-September through early November.

Vineyard production: Five acres of fruit trees containing eight exotic varieties pears, including Hosui, Yoi Nashi, and Shinko pear along with Fuji Apple produce seven-hundred cases annually. All wine is made from estate grown fruit.

Facility: Entails a wealth of outbuildings for processing the fruit. While the owners are warm and welcoming, no wine is for sale and no tastings or events are available at time. Instead, find Chestnut Run Farm wines at local stores, and all Garden State Wine Growers Festivals.

Directions: By your favorite method, get onto Route I-295 and proceed to Exit 4, taking Route 40 southeast. Proceed on Route 40 through Woodstown, past East Lake Road, and turn left onto Stewart Road. The winery is about a half mile up, on your right.

CODA ROSSA WINERY

1525 Dutch Mill Road, Franklinville, NJ 08322
856-424-9463, info@codarossa.com
www.codarossawinery.com

Owner: Kenton & Kathy Nice
Winemaker: Kenton Nice

Public hours: *All year:* weekends, 12ᴾᴹ–5ᴾᴹ, or by appointment. **(Free tastings.)**

Events: None held at the winery, but a host of events are at owners' custom-grape pressing shop: The Wine Room in Cherry Hill. Those trampling their own grapes may join in festivities ranging from the Chilean Crush Celebration to Murder Mystery Nights (visit www.thewineroom.com).

Description: For those who have swirled the vintages, toured the vineyards, and witnessed the experts performing their harvest-time magic, Coda Rossa offers oenophiles one step further—literally. CPA Ken Nice's and psychologist wife Kathy's desire to share their love of wine led them to launch The Wine Room in Cherry Hill in 2002. Here is a chance to get your feet wet in the full operation of making your personal wine. Visitors purchase the grapes and are guided through the processing steps using the latest, most fun equipment in the eight-thousand square-foot, Tuscan-designed Wine Room plant. Your blend, your label.

Yet if you do "stomp" by, be sure to sample the Coda Rossa Winery vintages which will doubtless draw you forty minutes east to the Nices' own vineyard and tasting room. The twelve-acres of diligently-tended, low-yield vines, though only producing since 2007, have yielded a selection of impressively full-bodied wines. Taking a glass of Cabernet Sauvignon or Super Tuscan and strolling among the remarkably hearty, young vines immediately out back gives a full sense of the Outer Coastal Plains benefits.

Be sure not to miss what Ken Nice terms Coda Rossa's whimsical side. The Changria, Picnogrigio, Raspberry Rosé, and Bluedonnay, a refreshing change of pace made from pure Garden State blueberries. As the Philadelphia Phillies were taking their triumphal parade to celebrate their World Series victory, avid fan Ken was bottling his custom Phillies Phinest Merlot (appropriately red.) At last, a vintner who crushes according to the will of the people.

Owner's most prized & favored wines:
Super Tuscany, $15
Rhone Style Syrah, $15
Cabernet Blend, $22
(Plus eight other offerings including Bluedonnay, Cabernet Sauvignon, Merlot, Nebbiolo, and Neve.)

Awards: No entries made in competitions.

Harvest season: Varieties are harvested mid-September through late October.

Vineyard production: Twelve acres containing seven varieties: Cabernet Franc, Cabernet Sauvignon, Chambourcin, Merlot, Sangiovese, Syrah, and Vidal, producing five-thousand cases annually. Some grapes are purchased from California, Chile, and Italy for blending.

Facility: A new, airy and broad tasting room stands at the vineyard. Forty miles west, in Cherry Hill, the Nices' eight-thousand square-foot The Wine Room in Cherry Hill stands decorated in Tuscany style with custom processing facilities and a restaurant serving Italian cuisine.

Directions: From Route I-295, in the north, or from the Millville or Vineland in the south, get onto Route 55. Just north of Vineland, at the jct. of Route 55, and at the jct. of Route 55 and Route 538, take Route 538 East (left) and then fairly quickly fork right onto Route 47 South (Delsea Drive). Just as Route 47 forks away to the right, stay straight on Route 40. Very shortly thereafter, turn left onto Dutch Mill Road. Proceed a few minutes up to the winery on your right.

Part of a common weekend Wine Trail including Amalthea, Coda Rossa, and Valenzano wineries.

CREAM RIDGE WINERY

145 Route 539, P.O. Box 98, Cream Ridge, NJ 08514
609-259-9797, crwinery@creamridgewinery.com
www.creamridgewinery.com

Retired Founders: Tom and Joan Amabile
Current CEO: Daughter Eileen Amabile
Winemaker: Brian Mulligan (Eileen's son)

Public hours: *All year:* Monday to Saturday, 11ᴬᴹ–6ᴾᴹ; Sunday, 11ᴬᴹ–5ᴾᴹ. **(Free tastings.)**

Events: Free tours during weekends. Special Wine Releases eleven months of the year (e.g. Chambourcin and Black Currant in October). Late March Fiesta Benefit for The Foundation for the Assistance of Abandoned Children (FANA). A Taste of Italy Anniversary Open House with live music & gourmet food. Country Roads 5K Run/Walk benefitting Allies, Inc. Plus several food festivals including a Holiday Open House and the September Bluegrass Music & Pig Roast. Large private tastings for $10 a head include tour samples with appropriate cheeses.)

Description: Part of the answer may be their warm welcome. Part may lie in their unusual array of fruit wines and traditional grape vintages. Yet for the last twenty years, folks have been happening upon Central Jersey's Cream Ridge, and loyally adopting it as their own.
    Set somewhat unexpectedly amid adjacent golf course, open parks, and sub-urban lots, this bastion of old farmland stands as a refreshing lure. The wide vine rows, large barrels, and homey, porched tasting building have inspired many to enter cautiously, sip, and smile with delight. For some, it's the dry, richly oaked Pinot Noir. For others it's the nectar-sweet Apricot wine.

The building has stood for more than two decades, shortly after the first vines were planted in 1988. Tom and Joan Amabile, leaving their Pennsylvania winery, purchased this property (aged barrels included) and plunged into wine making full time. A hand of Fate? Years later, daughter Eileen (Cream Ridge's owner after Tom's 1997 retirement) was rummaging in the basement. She unearthed a painting done by Tom during his high school days in Brooklyn—an exact likeness of today's winery. (See it when you visit.)

Whatever your premonitory perceptions, there's no speculation required for Cream Ridge's offerings. A fruit wine lover's haven, original Garden State tastes, such as Black Currant, Almond Berry, Chocolate Berry (blackberry), and Plum have been added to the more conventional Blueberry, Strawberry, and Cherry. Most of these vintages are available year round, but try to schedule your pilgrimages during release weekends. The festivity gives each new taste a definite edge.

Owner's most prized & favored wines:
Cherry, (Ciliegia Amabile), $14.95
Cabernet Sauvignon, $19.95
Cream Ridge Red, $13.95
Cranberry (All Jersey Fruit), $14.95
(Plus ten other offerings including a dry Pinot Gris, and semidry Riesling, and such original fruit wines as Almondberry, Black Currant, Chocolateberry.)

Awards include: Six New Jersey Governor's Cups for Cherry, Plum, and Cranberry.

Harvest season: Varieties are harvested from the end of August through September.

Vineyard production: Fourteen acres containing Cabernet Franc, Chambourcin, Dehaunic, Fredonia, and Lemberger varieties, and beach plums. This produces five-thousand cases annually. A portion of grapes are purchased from east coast and California vineyards.

Facility: Pleasant tasting room and dining facilities that seat forty. In the warmer months, airy tents provide for larger, catered parties.

Directions: *From North or South* on the NJ Turnpike. take Exit 7A and bear right onto I-195 East towards Six Flags Park. Take I-195 Exit 8 onto Route 539 South to Allentown. Ignore bypass sign for Rt. 539, staying straight on Rt. 539 South (will turn into Main Street). In Allentown you will pass the Black Forest Restaurant located in the Old Mill on the right. After crossing the bridge, 539 makes a sharp left, (High Street). Winery is 3.0 miles on right.
From the East and Shore Points, take I-195 West towards Trenton, get off at Exit 16 on to Route 537 West, towards Six Flags Park. Pass Great Adventure, and make a right hand turn at the light onto Route 539 North towards Allentown. After the Cream Ridge Golf Course (on left), take first left turn, staying on Rt. 539 North. The Winery is the first building on left, past the golf course.

Part of the Central Jersey Wine Trail, including Cream Ridge, 4JG's, and Silver Decoy vineyards.

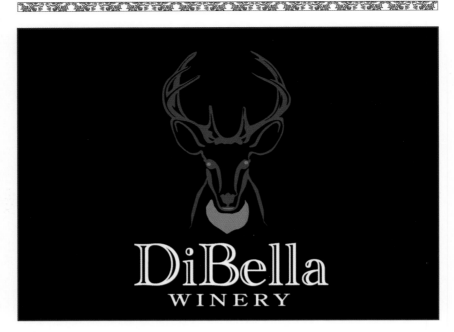

DiBella Winery

229 Davidson Road, Woolwich Twp. NJ 08085
856-467-0288, dibellawinery@yahoo.com

Owner: Will and Julie DiBella
Winemaker: Will DiBella

Public hours: No tasting room, but look for one in 2011. Visitors are always welcome. Please call ahead. Wines may be purchased at all New Jersey Wine Festivals, J.B. Liquors in Swedesboro; Hops and Grain in Glassboro; and Joe Canal's Liquors. Call winery for purchasing arrangements.

Events: Autumn Harvest Picking Festival in which food, wine and music piped through the fields accompany the joyful labors of the visitors.

Description: No, it doesn't taste like a Cabernet Franc from a winery that just corked its first bottles in 2008. The rich dark color portends the full, fruity flavor with a dry finish which makes it the ideal companion to fine cheese and fireside on a winter's eve. But the young couple who launched this young winery on a modest four acres present a deceptive picture. There's nothing novice here.

Will DiBella and his brother Alfred are fourth generation farmers who grew up on their homestead raising every imaginable crop grown in the Garden State. In 1925, Will's great grandfather, a recent immigrant from Italy, quit his beer delivery job and bought the farm which has expanded to the 250 planted acres the DiBellas work today.

As his Dad grew ill and less able to tend the soybeans, Will's hopes turned toward wine grapes. "I wanted something I could pass on to my family," he says. A timely idea, since wife Julie has just given birth to their lovely daughter Gia shortly after their first harvest.

The vines, like their owners, hold more experience than anticipated. In 2002, Will and Alfred planted their first acres with Merlot. Using widely spaced, heavily sodded rows, DiBella produced grapes of a quality exceptional enough to meet the purchasing standards of Heritage Vineyards. Experimentation continues, and today DiBella precision-tended plots embrace seven different varieties.

The optimal environs for sampling DiBella's surprisingly full semidry Pinot Grigio is amidst their Autumn Harvest, in which Julie sets out barbecue and wines, and Will's baritone serenades the laborers.

Owner's most prized & favored wines:
> Traminette 2008, $11.50
> Merlot 2008, $14.95
> Pinot Grigio 2008, $12.50
> Cabernet Franc 2008, $14.95

(Plus two new offerings: a Cherry Cordial and Raspberry Merlot.)

Awards: No entries made in competitions as of yet.

Harvest season: Varieties are harvested early-September through mid-October.

Vineyard production: Four acres containing Cabernet Franc, Cabernet Sauvignon, Chardonnay, Lemberger, Pinot Grigio, Merlot, and Traminette varieties and producing 250 cases annually. All wines are from estate grown grapes, and DiBella even sells some of its fruit to other Garden State wineries.

Facility: All the winemaking takes place in innovatively arranged sheds out back, but watch for the tasting room which is soon to come in their future.

Directions: *From the North,* take the NJ Turnpike to Exit 2, turning left onto Route 322 West at the end of the ramp. Proceed to Kings Highway (Route 551) and take it left a short ways. Then turn left onto Route 538 and follow it, veering right as it becomes Route 694. Take Route 694 to Russell Road, and make a right. Look for Davidson Road on your right almost immediately. Turn right onto Davidson and the winery is a short ways up on your right.

Part of a common Gloucester County Wine Trail, including Auburn Road, Cedarvale, DiBella, Heritage, and Wagonhouse vineyards.

DiMatteo Vineyards

779 11th Street, Hammonton, NJ 08037
609-605-9700 or 567-3909, dimatteowine@wildblue.net
www.dimatteowinery.com

Owner: Frank DiMatteo, Sr. & Frank DiMatteo, Jr.
Winemaker: Frank DiMatteo, Sr.
Vintner: Frank DiMatteo, Jr.

Public hours: *All year:* Saturday and Sunday, 12ᴾᴹ–5ᴾᴹ. **(Free tastings.)**

Events: Instructive tours by owners during public hours. Also, a video offers a virtual tour of the vineyard and winery for rainy days.

Description: Like any good Italian family, the DiMatteos believe that fine wine enhances both food and life. Swing by this Outer Coastal Plain winery, and you will feel the natural hospitality as if borne in on the lowland breezes. Frank Sr. and Frank Jr. (III) truly treat each visitor as welcome guest, and they will gladly drop all else to explain how their smooth, full bodied Chambourcin enlivens beef tenderloin or rack of lamb. Here is your destination to learn about pairing wine with food.

The modest tasting room is currently under expansion, but it is out in the vineyard where you want to tour. Follow Frank Jr. up the gentle rise, gaze down on the avenues of vines below. Listen as he tells why the Fredonia is placed nearby and the Ives, lower down. Career farmer Frank Jr. first transformed his vegetable acreage into vines in 1999 and became a vintner. Frank Sr., recently construction firm owner, came on as inside man to handle winery and sales duties. Anxious to improve on a dubious family tradition, Frank Sr. recalls scrubbing the barrels and processing his grandmother's "not overly agreeable" wine which sold to neighbors like hot cakes.

Today, in the winery's four locales, the DiMatteos have achieved their dreams of quality. Try the refreshingly light Diamond white in their back room. Or sit out under the arbor and sample the signature Pasquale Red. This unique blend of Concord and Ives is precisely created for Italian foods. You'll agree.

Owner's most prized & favored wines:

Pasquale Red, $10
Cranberry, $10.95
Chambourcin 2006, $12.95
Strawberry, $9

(Plus eleven other offerings including a Traminette, and Jersey White blend, plus four fruit wines, including Plum.)

Awards include: 2009 NJ Wine Growers Association Gold: Strawberry; Silver: Pasquale Red, Cabernet Franc; Bronze: Diamond and Niagara.

Harvest season: Varieties are harvested end of August through 3rd week in October. (No harvest festival.)

Vineyard production: Fourteen-and-one-half acres containing twelve varieties, including Chambourcin, Chancellor, Concord, Fredonia, Ives, Merlot, Niagara, Syrah, Traminette, and Vidal Blanc, producing 1,500 cases annually. Some grapes sold to other Garden State vineyards.

Facility: Small tasting room, but look forward to a new room and expanded quarters soon. Larger barrel room for private parties. An inviting arbor for picnics.

Directions: *From the Atlantic City Expressway,* take Exit 29 onto Route 54 North (12th Street.) Proceed a short ways to Second Road, take it right, then turn left onto Eleventh Street. The winery entrance sign is a short way up.

From the North, using your favorite method, get onto Route 206 South, taking it to Hammonton where it becomes Route 54 South. Proceed through the town. Turn left onto South Second Road, then left onto Eleventh Street.

Part of the Hammonton Wine Trail, DiMatteo, Pllagido's, Sharrott, and Tomasello vineyards.

FOUR SISTERS WINERY

783 County Route 519, Belvidere, NJ 07823
908-475-3671, foursisterswinery@gmail.com
www.foursisterswinery.com

Owners: Matty and Laurie Matarazzo
Winemaker: Matty Matarazzo

Public hours: *All year:* Thursday through Tuesday, 11^AM–6^PM. **(Complete tastings are free.)**

Events: Free scheduled tours during set hours on festival days. Murder Mystery Nights with dinner and wine in the Vintners Room. Comedy Nights with wine and dinner under the party tent. Harvest Festival and Pig Roasts—September and October. Family Fun Days with hay rides, corn maze, pick your own pumpkins and apples. Barefoot Grape Stomping and Cellar Tour. St. Patrick Early Release Wine Tasting.

Description: "Farming is not like other jobs, it's a lifestyle. It's like a tree with branches. The love of the land does not come from the heart itself, it runs through every vein in our bodies" explains Four Sisters Manager Valerie Tishuk. Witness the love by watching third generation farmer and winery founder, Matty Matarazzo and wife Laurie working throughout their 250-acre farm. Their fruits and vegetables have delighted North Jerseyians since 1921.

Passing through the country gift shop on your way to the cedar-scented tasting room, pause and sample the cornucopia of fruit jellies and rich breads. You will then be ready to experience the fullness of their estate-grown Matty's

---

Apple Port, Pumpkin wine or Leon Millot Reserve. Wander out back with a glass of Papa's Red (a unique blend created by Matty's Dad), across the steep slopes and sylvan vista of the Warren Hills. This region imbues Matty's grapes with the moist lime soil and ample sunlight found in Burgundy, France.

In 1984, Matty and wife Laurie realized their four daughters, Melissa, Serena, Robin, and Sadie were all going to require educations. So, in 1984, when two-year-old Sadie was just small enough to nap in wine cases, Matty made a farmer's ideal investment: eight acres of grapes, which have now seen all his ladies through college.

Today, the Matarazzo clan has distilled the crushing labor of farming into an enjoyable family experience. They celebrate everything from Saint Patrick's to Saint Swithin's with family hayrides, Mystery Nights, Comedy Nights and pig roasts. Take your choice. Enjoy a day at the farm.

Owner's most prized & favored wines:
Beaver Creek Red, $14
Niagara, $12.95
Papa's Red, $12.95
Cayuga, $12.95
(Plus twelve other offerings including Maggie's Magic Champagne, two Ports, Apple, Cherry, Strawberry, Raspberry fruit wines.)

Awards include: 2008 Wine Growers Association Gold. State and International competition Gold: Cayuga, Niagara , Seyval Reserve; Silver: Vidal Blanc Papa's Red, Beaver Creek Red, Holiday Seasoned. Bronze; Warren Hills White, Cedar Hills White.

Harvest season: Varieties are harvested late August through mid-October.

Vineyard production: The eight acres of grapes and seven acres of orchard contain twelve varieties of apples and ten varieties of grapes, including cold hardy, less common Frontenac and Leon Millot. Another sixty percent of their grapes (mostly Niagara and Concord,) are purchased from regional vineyards. These produce approximately 4,200 cases annually.

Facility: The country gift shop, leading to the cozy, cedar tasting room, carries an array of jellies, cheeses, fruits and breads. The back deck overlooks the vineyard and Warren Hills. Event dinners are held in the larger Vintner's Room, or in warmer weather, in the spacious party tent.

Directions: *From Route I-80,* take Exit 12. At the bottom of the ramp, turn left, the winery is six miles down on the right.

From Route I-78, take Exit 13 onto Route 31 North. At its end, turn left onto Route 46 West. At the first traffic light, turn right onto Route 519 North. The winery is two miles up on the left.

Part of the Warren Hills Wine Trail, including Alba, Brook Hollow, Four Sisters, and Villa Milagro Vineyards.

HAWK HAVEN VINEYARD & WINERY

600 S. Railroad Avenue, Rio Grande, NJ 08242
609-846-7347, info@hawkhavenvineyard.com
www.hawkhavenvineyard.com

Owner: Todd & Kenna Wuerker
Winemaker: Todd Wuerker

Public hours: Winter: every day, 11ᴬᴹ to 6ᴾᴹ; Summer: every day, 11ᴬᴹ to 7ᴾᴹ.
($5 affords five tastings and souvenir glass for $2.)

Events: Fall & Winter Friday Night Dining in the Barrel Room: the food comes from local Cape May Restaurants, local jazz groups enliven the evening from 6:30ᴾᴹ to 10ᴾᴹ; reservations required. Sangria Sundays begin 4ᴾᴹ from Memorial Day through Labor Day weekends.

The Cape May Wine Train runs weekends from Victorian City to Hawk Haven, and allows visitors to see the shore, and enjoy a box lunch with wine at Hawk Haven.

Description: The doors have just flung wide on Memorial Day 2011, and the obviously new, warmly paneled tasting room may set your palate to accept first-season efforts. Then comes the surprise. The wrist-thick vines out back have basked under the nearby ocean's breezes since their first planting in 1997. Back in the tasting room, the complexity of 2007 Merlot and the rich, full finish of the Cabernet Sauvignon bear testimony to this maturity.

Before coming into their own, Hawk Haven founders Todd Wuerker and wife Kenna produced the twelve varieties on their nine-acre vineyard for five other South Jersey wineries. Following in the tradition of his grandfather and father, who owned and tilled this land since 1940, Todd is a careful, precise farmer. When he set aside the vineyard from the 110 acres of pumpkins and lima beans, he designed a strategy for long term development. His restricted space planting brings less fruit on each vine, less fruit per acre—and more quality.

It is this blend of generational farm wisdom, and a refreshing, energetic approach that have developed their 2007 American Kestrel White. This lightly oaked Chardonnay subtly enhances rather than overwhelms seafood. Likewise, Hawk Haven's 2008 Riesling holds a surprisingly full body without being cloyingly sweet.

Here is your chance to walk, picnic, and explore. Like the hawks overhead, visitors may roam the vineyard's one-hundred acres, find one of the tree-hemmed lakes, and perhaps settle in with a 2008 Pinot Grigio for lunch. My personal favorite: a sip on the old-fashioned rope swing out front.

Owner's most prized & favored Wines:
Merlot, $32
Cabernet Sauvignon, $28
Red Table Wine, $19
Pinot Grigio, $19
(Plus four other offerings, including a newly released Chardonnay for $14.)

Harvest season: Varieties are harvested mid-September through end of October.

Vineyard production: Nine-plus acres containing twelve varieties, such as Syrah, Cabernet Franc, Malbec, Merlot, Riesling and the black Spanish Tempranillo. These plus twenty percent of grapes bought locally produce two-thousand cases annually.

Facility: The ample Wine Room with long tasting bar hold fifty joyful oenophiles easily. The barrel room offers intimate parties the right atmosphere for dinner and elegant evenings. Outside, Hawk Haven invites guests to wander the over ten-acres with lakes and natural picnic areas, and also offers a twenty-five-person tent to serve as party central.

Directions: *By road:* Take the Garden State Parkway to Exit 4 (Rio Grande) and continue on Route 47 North. At the third, traffic light, turn left onto Railroad Avenue. The winery is 3/4 miles up on the left.
From the Cape May Ferry, Exit straight out of ferry parking lot. At fourth traffic light (Seashore Road) turn left and proceed north 3.5 miles. Winery is on left.

Part of the Cape May Wine Trail, including Cape May, Hawk Haven, Natali, and Turdo vineyards.

HERITAGE VINEYARDS

Heritage Station, 480 Mullica Hill Road, Mullica Hill, NJ 08062
856-589-4474, rich@heritagewinenj.com
www.heritagestationwine.com

Owners: Bill, Penni, and Richard Heritage
Winemaker: Bill Heritage

Public hours: *All year:* seven days a week, 9^{AM} to 6^{PM}; winery tours scheduled Saturdays, 1^{PM} and 3^{PM}. **(Free tastings.)**

Events: "Un-Wine" Happy Hour Tasting every Thursday 6 ^{PM}–9 ^{PM}. Live music the last Thursday each month. (June–October). Farm market and pick your own apples, pumpkins and pears in season. Autumn Cider Parties. Private birthday parties year round. Gently grassy knolls can and do accommodate thousands in statewide festivals.

Description: For the gourmet seeking the gauntlet of down-farm treats, a pilgrimage to Heritage truly fulfills. Cheeses, honeys, fruits—jammed, fresh, and canned—all flank the inviting wine tasting bar centered amidst a huge, enticing shop dedicated to your palate. Bill, Penni, and son Richard Heritage, a six-generation farm family, manage their 150 acres of Jersey fresh produce and run their store with a style that appeals.

Seen originally as a fiscal farm saver, Bill first turned twenty-acres to grapes in 1996. By Heritage Winery's 2001 opening, this plot netted income comparable to the ninety remaining acres of apples, peaches, and pears. Meanwhile, Penni's

---

small outdoor farm-stand had taken hold, aided by Richard's budding entrepreneurial ventures. Today, the stand has mushroomed into a landmark store boasting cheese bar, bakery and winery. Soon, the entire farm will be under vine with a range of exotic varietals.

Ever seeking to adapt unusual grapes such as Malbec and Grenache to this Outer Coastal region, Heritage begins new vines in the greenhouse. When ready, each is placed precisely on the steady, rolling slopes for best advantage—100 percent sun for the Syrah; cooler areas for the Sauvignon Blanc. Back in the winery, Bill selects from his collection of high to medium toast Pennsylvania oak barrels, making them a spice rack for his artful blends. Try the full-bodied Red Caboose and the Bordeaux-style Steel Rails Red.

Whether it's a three-thousand-guest tented soiree sipping popular Sweet Concord or Thursdays' "Un-Wine" Happy Hour with pulled pork and prize Chambourcin, Heritage warmly accommodates all.

Owner's most prized & favored wines:
Chambourcin 2007, $22.50
Cabernet Franc 2007, $24.50
Merlot 2007, $19.50
Estate Chardonnay 2006, $16.99
(Plus fourteen others. Varietals include Merlot, Cabernet Sauvignon, Cabernet Franc, Syrah, Petit Verdot, and Malbec.)

Awards include: 2005 Governor's Cup for Chambourcin

Harvest season: Varieties are harvested mid-October through mid-November.

Vineyard production: Twenty-five acres containing six varieties and producing 3,500 cases annually. All wine is from Heritage's own estate grapes.

Facility: Large tasting room within a fully stocked farm-produce market. Ample grassy acreage and tents and tables for outdoor picnics of all sizes. New banquet facility planned.

Directions: *From the South and Vineland area,* take Route 55 North. Turn left (West) on Route 322 West. Proceed 1 mile to Heritage Station.
From the North and Camden area, take Route 55 South. Turn right (West) on Route 322 West. Proceed 1 mile to Heritage Station.
From NJ Turnpike, take Exit 2 onto Route 322 East 7 miles into Richwood. See Heritage Winery on right.

Part of a common Wine Trail including including Auburn Road, Cedarville, Chestnut Run, Heritage, and Wagonhouse wineries..

HOPEWELL VALLEY VINEYARDS

46 Yard Road, Pennington, NJ 08534
609-737-4465, violettahvv@gmail.com
www.hopewellvalleyvineyards.com

Owners: Sergio & Violetta Neri
Winemaker: Sergio Neri

Public hours: *All year:* daily, 12^PM–5^PM; Friday, 12^PM–8^PM. **($5 affords six tastings and souvenir glass.)**

Events: Friday Happy Hours (5^PM–8^PM). Garden fresh vegetables, fruits, and herbs grown on vineyard acreage for sale in season. Three instructive courses: "Seed to Bottle," "The Art of Wine Tasting," and "Wines of the World." Also check site for frequent Music Nights with jazz, rock, and classical genres.

Description: Succumb to the ultimate in Greco-Roman hospitality. Both Sergio Neri in Italy, and wife Violetta in Macedonia came from winemaking families, who knew how to treat guests. With your glass of richly oaked Barbera, stroll down from the tasting room into the grand ballroom where you might find talented Sergio on the concert Steinway completing the mood. Come Friday eves, and witness both Violetta and Sergio tending their homemade pizza in the brick ovens.

Yet the Neris' real gift for hospitality lies in the labor of their wines. Achieving adequate subsoil percolation demanded Sergio's plowing his earth-gouging tractor 380 miles across his farm's acres to break up the Delaware Valley's hallmark shale/clay pan. He then planted his well drained Italian varietals in tight, (seven feet) European-style rows, some with only one fruiting cane, to encourage more fruit and root than foliage. As always, he teases the valley frosts, harvesting each variety on the last possible days, to achieve maximum sugar.

These strategies have proved themselves in the tasting. Sample Hopewell's noticeably fuller Chambourcin '06, their late-harvested Dolce Vita blend, and the unusual White Merlot (the vineyard's first grape.) Of course, to best experience the ties between Garden State and Tuscany vintages, ask about renting the Neri family villa in Castellina, Italy. Here, in the Chianti Classico region, the Neri family still owns a vineyard. Their villa stands elegantly with spacious rooms, pool, chef and maid service, and lush grounds, amidst a host of enticing vineyards. What a vacation for you and eleven close, adventurous friends.

Owner's most prized & favored wines:
Cabernet Sauvignon, $17.95
Sangiovese, $20.95
Chambourcin 2006, $17.95
Barbera, $16.95

(Plus twelve other offerings, including those from estate-grown Chardonnay, Pinot Griggio, Pinot Noir, Tramminette, and Vidal varieties.)

Awards include: 2009 Governor's Cup, Chambourcin 2006; Finger Lakes International Competition, Silver: Barbera; Atlantic Seaboard Wine Competition, Gold: Stony Brook Dry Blush, Silver: Roso Della Valle & Pinot Griggio; International Eastern Wine Competition, Gold: Porto Bianco, Silver: Cabernet Sauvignon and Merlot.

Harvest season: Varieties are harvested late September through early November.

Vineyard production: Twenty-five acres (twenty more coming) containing seven varieties and producing approximately six-thousand cases annually. Up to fifteen percent of grapes purchased from other vineyards, mostly local.

Facility: Tasting room with stone floors and bottles festively displayed, large enough for fifty leads to lofty banquet hall seating 130, with a stage for performances. Expansive deck out on front overlooks vineyards.

Directions: *From the South,* In central Jersey, take Route 295 North/95 South to Exit 4 onto Route 31 North. Continue on 31, 2.5 miles past Pennington Circle. Turn left onto Yard Road. Winery is 7/10 mile on left.

From the North, Take Route 202 South (or your optimal route) to Flemington Circle, and continue on Route 202/31 South for 6 miles. Take the exit onto 31 South and proceed another 7.5 miles to Yard Road. Turning right onto Yard Road, go 7/10 miles to winery on your left.

Part of a popular weekend Wine Trail, including Alba, Hopewell Valley, Silver Decoy and Unionville Vineyards.

LAURITA WINERY

35 Archertown Road, New Egypt, NJ 08533
609-758-8000, manager@lauritawinery.com
www.lauritawinery.com

Owner: Randy Johnson & Ray Shea
Winemaker: Nicolaas J. Opdam

Public hours: *All year:* Thursday–Monday, 12ᴾᴹ–9ᴾᴹ; Saturday, 12ᴾᴹ–5ᴾᴹ; Sunday, 12ᴾᴹ–7ᴾᴹ. **($7 affords six tastings and souvenir glass.)**

Events: Scheduled tours daily during public hours by foot or motor cart. (Reservations required. $250 for groups of up to twenty-five, tasting included & $10 for each additional person.) Hay rides. Pick-Your-Own fruits at adjacent farms. Frequent weekend band concerts (all size bands). Movie festivals. Farm bike Rides (rental available from adjacent Dancer Farm.) Horse riding lessons and trails at Laurita Equestrian Center.

Description: If any winery has earned the label of "a destination," it is Laurita. From what its founders, contractor Randy Johnson and attorney Ray Shea, term "a real estate deal gone bad," has risen the gracious Dancer Farm B&B, the Laurita Equestrian Center, the Healing Spirits Massage Spa, and the Rein Dancer Therapeutic Riding Center. All amidst hosts of pick-your-own farms.

Laurita's crown jewel is the palatial winery formed by the ingenious melding of two huge 150-year old barns. Wandering beneath the high, hand-adzed beams, stop at the old oaken, 1890 Kansas City bar, take a robust Cabernet Franc or Merlot, and stroll past classical statuary artfully mingled with avant murals.

On a more casual note, take your Beachcomber Blush or Tailgate Red out on the porch overlooking forty-four-acres of vines cum solar arrays. Food abounds, but do not miss the richly appointed cheese shop. Pairing wine with cheese is a Laurita specialty.

Touring the processing rooms below reveals winemaker Nick Opdam's Frankensteinian laboratory and a computerized vat control system rivaling anything in Napa. Among the few Garden State wineries to employ strictly Hungarian oak, Laurita's Chardonnays are unique.

Though Shea and Johnson first planted in 1999, and sold wine within six years, their current complex has just opened in September, 2008. Truly, it offers a gourmet weekend getaway. So instead of a theme-park fantasy, try the very real pleasures of Laurita. Centered on the celebration of wine, the senses and mind are delightfully indulged.

Owner's most prized & favored wines:
Merlot 2005, $28
Pinot Gris 2005, $18
Down the Shore Beachcomber Blush, $15
Chardonnay Reserve, $22
(Plus thirteen other offerings including an oakless "Naked Chardonnay," Zweigelt, Lemberger, and fruity Bistro.)

Awards include: Florida State Fair Wine Competition Gold: Chambourcin; Silver: Lemberger; Bronze: Pinot Gris.

Harvest season: Varieties are harvested mid-September through late October.

Vineyard production: Forty-four acres of grapes, containing Cabernet Franc, Cabernet Sauvignon, Chardonnay, Chambourcin, Lemberger, Merlot, Norton, Pinot Gris and Zweigelt varieties and producing fourteen-thousand cases annually. All wines are from estate grown grapes.

Facility: A massive two level wine and food emporium of two-plus, high-ceilinged stories, with appropriate decks overlooking the vineyard. Inside are several tasting bars, a fromagerie, food areas with several types of cuisine. Party and dance spaces on each floor.

Directions: *From the South,* proceed to the junction of Routes 70 and 539 and take 539 North, through Fort Dix, as it becomes Pinehurst Road. Turn left on West Colliers Mill Road. Just under a mile, Colliers Mills turns sharply right becoming Archertown Road, which then curves sharply left. The Winery is just after this S-curve.

From the NJ Turnpike, take Exit 7A onto Interstate 195 East. Take Exit 7 to Route 526 East (Allentown). Go through town and after passing a mill pond, turn left onto Route 539 South (High Street). Proceed on Route 539 and turn right onto West Colliers Mill and proceed as above.

From the Garden State Parkway, take Exit 98 for Interstate I-195 West, and take exit 16 (Mount Holly). Follow Monmouth Road (Route 537) 3.3 miles to the first traffic light after Great Adventure, and turn left onto Route 539 South and proceed as above.

Part of Central Jersey Wine Trail, including Cream Ridge, Laurita, and Silver Decoy Vineyards.

NATALI VINEYARDS

221 North Delsea Drive (North Rt. 47,)
Cape May Courthouse, NJ 08201
609-465-0075, chazrayp@dotnet.com
www.natalivineyards.com

Owners: Al Natali, Ray Pensari, Tony Antonelli

Public hours: *All year:* daily, 11 ᴬᴹ–5 ᴾᴹ. October: Harvest events. **($5 affords complete tastings.)**

Events: Free tours daily during public hours. Live music festivals.

Description: Take the long, curving, tree-lined drive into Al, Ray, and Tony's vineyard, and you feel you've stepped back into an old world farm winery. Seated and sipping beneath the vine-shaded trellis, one savors the steady, ocean-borne breeze which dries and enriches the acres of fruit stretching toward the horizon.

No frills, no gift shop—simply a place to enjoy the wine and other products grown around this Outer Coastal Plain region. This is exactly what the owners intended from the start. For all three successful businessmen, the winery was to be a bold stride toward a more fulfilling kind of success. ADP executive, Al Natali sort of wanted to sell his long-held seventy acres to large-scale developers Ray Pensari and Tony Antonelli. But not really. After some chatting in 2000, the three decided a winery would better suit their purposes—and souls.

Like any good owner, Al knew the true value of his land. The sandy soils of New Jersey's southern finger epitomize the Outer Coastal Plain's similarity to France's Bordeaux region. Thus in 2001, Natali planted accordingly his first six acres with thirteen varieties of Bordeaux-adaptable vines. The result has been a list of delightful dry reds and whites. In keeping with his location just a half mile off Delaware Bay, the vineyard also offers a blueberry and beach plum.

Partake in the pleasures of Meadow's Edge (Ray's Great Granddad's recipe) when the farmer's market with live jazz music comes to join in. Casual, tasty & fun.

Owner's most prized & favored wines:
Meadow's Edge, $16
Blueberry, $16
Cabernet Sauvignon 2007, $18
Cedar Hammock, $16

(Plus ten other grape varieties, locally harvested, including their own beach plum wine.)

Awards include: 2009 Wine Growers Association award winners: Viogner, Shiraz, Dolcetto.

Harvest season: Varieties are harvested early September through late through October.

Vineyard production: Nearly ten acres containing five varieties and producing one-thousand cases annually. A small percentage of grapes are purchased from California vineyards for Meadow's Edge blend.

Facility: Full tasting room, shaded patio, deck, ample outside space and tents for all occasions.

Directions: 221 Delsea Drive is Route 47 North and the Winery is near milepost 12.9. Look for the Natali Vineyards sign. The winery is about 800 feet up the drive on left. (You may approach Route 47 from the north by taking the G.S. Parkway South below exit 10B. Turn right on East Mechanic Street, right onto Goshen Road, left on Williams Street, then left on Route 47 South.)

Part of the Cape May Wine Trail, including Cape May, Hawk Haven, Natali, and Turdo Vineyards.

OLD YORK CELLARS

80 Old York Road, Ringoes, NJ 08551
908-284-9463, scott@oldyorkcellars.com
www.oldyorkcellars.com

Owner: David S. Wolin
Winemaker: Scott Gares

Public hours: *All year:* Friday through Sunday, 12^{PM}–5 ^{PM}. **($5 affords complete tastings. $7.50 includes a souvenir glass.)**

Events: Tours daily during public hours through vineyard by appointment. Wine and Food Series, with Chef Andrew Pandano and others instructing and performing their art. Release dates for Case Club buyers. (Look for more coming from this new winery under the skillful hands of events manager, Laurin Dormin.)

Description: Marianne Gares (Mom to winemaker, Scott), ever urges guests to take bottle and glass, and push through the double doors onto the broad stone patio. From there, wander down amidst the vineyard rows carved out, so many years ago, from the forested Sourland Hills. Marianne has poured fine Chardonnays from this winery back when it bore the Amwell Valley name. Loyal guests return annually to savor both the vintages and atmosphere produced by these lush, rolling slopes.

Just outside the finely paneled tasting room, the thigh-thick vines boasting young, bud-laden shoots form a perfect metaphor for this rejuvenated winery. After several decades of devotion, Amwell Valley Vineyards' Mike Fisher passed on, and the vineyard fell into neglect. Yet Fisher had created a talented legacy in Scott Gares who embraced his mentor's skills, and added his own artistry.

Meanwhile, real estate attorney David Wolin was visiting Mendoza, Argentina's vineyards. He returned with a love of Malbec grape—and an idea. Their creation of Old York formed an ideal match. Wolin brought the cash, wine enthusiasm, and business sense. Gares contributed immense winemaking skills, and an army of local family and friends to help.

After the 2008 purchase, they planted six-hundred new vines, erected all new posts and wires, and harvested their initial crop from the disastrous 2009 season. Unique to the Garden State, they experimented with Landot Noir, and other cold-hearty grapes. The result is a growing selection of popular Pinot Griggio, an intense, full-finished Malbec, and others reflecting the best of the new grafted onto the most enduring of the old.

Owner's most prized & favored wines:
Pinot Griggio, $17.50
Syrah, $17.50
Merlot, $16.50
Cabernet Sauvignon, $19.50
(Plus six other offerings including Chardonnay, Landot Noir—on the way, a dry and a sweet Riesling, Malbec, and Vidal Blanc. Also, next season, look for Blackberry, Blush, Peach, and Vintners Blend of Malbec, Merlot, and Syrah.)

Awards include: No wines entered yet.

Harvest season: Varieties are harvested early September through early October.

Vineyard production: Twelve of its twenty-seven acres are under vine and contain old and new grape varieties, including, Cabernet Sauvignon, Chardonnay, Landot Noir, Malbec, Merlot, Pinot Griggio, Riesling, Syrah varieties. For their first season, following a great crop devastation, much of the 2009 grapes were purchased, but 2010 and onward should be mostly estate grown.

Facility: A mid-size tasting room opens onto the gracious stone patio overlooking the sweep of this Sourlands vineyard. Across the road a larger hall can handle parties up to sixty guests.

Directions: *From the North.* Using your favorite method, get onto Route 202/206 South. This may be taking the NJ Turnpike, exiting at #10 onto I-287 North, then I-287 North's exit 14 onto Route 22 West, leading to Route 202/206 South. Or it may involve coming South on 287, (just above its junction with I-78) and taking exit 22 onto Route 202/206 South.
Either way, from there follow Route 202 South, after it splits from Route 206. Shortly after 202 joins Route 31, follow it across Route 514. Just after Route 604 enters from the right, go 1/4 mile and turn left on Old York Road. The Winery is a short way up on the right.
From the South. Taking Route 202 North from anywhere beyond Lambertville, or Route 31 North from anywhere out of Ewing area, follow either route. Shortly after they join, look for Route 179 which is Old York Road. Take Old York north—right—and the winery is a short ways up on the right. Or you can pick up Old York Road in Ringoes center. As you enter town, and bypass the Route 202 turnoff, get onto Route 179/Route 31 North. The winery is 4.5 miles up from town on the right.

Part of the Central Jersey Wine Trail, including Cream Ridge, Old York Cellars, Silver Decoy, Terhune, and Unionville Vineyards.

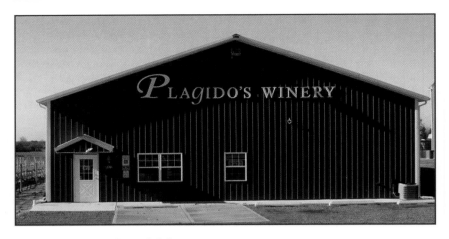

PLAGIDO'S WINERY

570 N. First Road, Hammonton, NJ 08037
609-567-4633, ollie@plagidoswinery.com
www.plagidoswinery.com

Owner: Ollie M. Tomasello
Winemaker: Ollie M. Tomasello

Public hours: *All year:* daily from 12ᴾᴹ–5 ᴾᴹ. **(Free tastings.)**

Events: Daily tours daily during public hours. Dinner shows with food, wine, and music from decades past and present.

Description: It is very alluring to move straight from the short, roadside drive into the intimate, warmly paneled Plagido tasting room. Friends and Tomassello family members greet guests and pour their rich oaked Chardonnay and Merlot reserve, as well as the Plagido Red, Cranberry wine, and special Sangria for the sweeter palates. Little wonder that area bicyclists and shoreward tourists alter their routes to include a sampling from Plagido's slightly overwhelming array of twenty-seven quite diverse wines.

But keeping inside would miss one of Plagido's most delightful features. Leave the tasting room and walk around the building's left side. Pass the low rows of Cabernet Franc on your left, and settle into the broad and shady apron out back. Adjust your small table and chair to take in the eye-level vineyard vista. A wide, unbroken river of seemingly endless vineage leads your eyes, thoughts, and cares to distant horizons along alternating lanes of soft, beige soils and lush, green columns of vine. Swirl your glass of impressively fruity Niagara, soak in the silence, and reflect.

In 1870, Italian immigrant Plagido Tomasello (no relation to nearby Tomasello Winery) pioneered and plowed these well-drained soils around burgeoning Hammonton village. A small vineyard provided for experimentation and family consumption. In 1999, grandson Ollie Senior and great-grandson Ollie Junior, transformed the two fourteen-acre plots from peaches into a full vineyard with nine varietals. As of August 1, 2009, Plagido's celebrates its third anniversary. When visiting, ask for a free vineyard tour, if only to walk and experience this verdant realm.

Owner's most prized & favored wines:
Plagido Red, $9.99
Antonia Rosso, $10.99
Concetta's Casalinga, $12.99
Plagido's Choice, $16.99
(Plus twenty-four other offerings, including oaked and unoaked Cabernets and Merlots, a Cabernet Franc Bianco, Plagido's own Sangria, and four fruit wines—including Peach.)

Awards include: 2009 Governor's Cup for their Cranberry; New Jersey Wine Growers Association Gold: Cabernet Franc and Antonia Rosso—also voted Best American Varietal 2008; Silver: Concetta's Casalinga and Cabernet Franc Reserve; Bronze Chardonnay,Cabernet-Merlot Blend, Cabernet Sauvignon.

Harvest season: Varieties are harvested late August through early November.

Vineyard production: Fourteen acres of vines containing nine varieties, including Cabernet Franc, Cabernet Sauvignon Chardonnay Chambourcin, Concord, Fredonia, Merlot, and Vidal Blanc producing three-thousand cases annually. All wine comes from estate grapes; fruit for fruit wines is purchased from local farms.

Facility: Cozy tasting room. Pleasant veranda out back with tables and view of vineyard.

Directions: *From the North,* By your favorite method (e.g. Route I-295 in Bordentown) get onto Route 206 South and proceed into Hammonton. At the junction with Route 30, Route 206 becomes Route 54. Take that (also called "12th Street") through Hammonton center, and turn right onto First Street. Winery is .6 mile on left.
   From the South, Connect with Route 54 North via Route 56 in Vineland or Route 322 a ways to the north. Proceed on Route 54 North into Hammonton and look for First Road. Turn left on First Road and go .6 mile to the winery on the left. From the Atlantic City Expressway, Take Exit 28 onto Route 54 North and proceed 1.6 miles up to First Road and turn left.

Part of the Hammonton Area Wine Trail, including DiMatteo, Plagido, Sharrott, and Tomasello Vineyards.

RENAULT WINERY

72 North Bremen Avenue,
Egg Harbor City, NJ 08215
609-965-2111, dave@renaultwinery.com
www.renaultwinery.com

Owner: Joseph Milza
Winemaker: David Memarscio; **Assistant winemaker:** Marco Bucchi

Public hours: *All year:* Sunday–Thursday, 10^AM^–5^PM^; Friday, 10^AM^–7^PM^ (Summers close at 5^PM^); Saturday, 10^AM^–8^PM^. **($3 tour of winery and includes free tasting.)**

Events: Scheduled free tours daily during public hours, mostly every hour. Brunch and dinner available at gourmet restaurants. Frequent golf tournaments on Renault's course. Seasonal holiday discount events at Tuscany House Hotel. Barefoot grape stomping during September and October harvests.

Description: Follow the graveled pathways through the tea-garden, past the gourmet restaurant, bake shop, and Tuscany House. Play the 7200-yard golf course of New Jersey's oldest winery, and you will see why Renault justifiably labels itself a Winery Resort. Geographically and atmospherically closest to Atlantic City, here is an excellent stage for novices to launch their initial wine explorations.

    The half-hour guided tour takes mid-size groups all through the processing plant, explaining each step of the creation found in Renault's exceptionally wide-ranging wine selection. (Here's your chance to behold two-thousand and four-thousand-gallon wooden vats still in use, and hand-grind champagne corkers.)

    When Louis Nicholas Renault first planted his vines in 1870, he brought with him a lifetime of winemaking experience in France's Champagne region, and five sons. The family carried on the winery until the death of Marie Renault in 1972, at the age of 101. In 1977 Joseph Milza seized this opportunity, bought, and gradually expanded the facility into today's wine resort.

The tour ends with a guided sampling in the dark, uniquely paneled tasting sanctuary. Though the cups are plastic, the pours are generous in number and explanation. The clever couple-pairing of wines shows winemaker Dave Demarscio's art to best advantage.

Reserve a sitting at the restaurant's six-course gourmet dinner, and you might sample his handiwork in the Noah (a colonial American original grape) or Renault's own Pink Lady. Save their hallmark Sparkling Wines for the Sunday Brunch. Then, for a full understanding, take a round of golf and witness the carefully intermingled vineyards to see where it all begins.

Owner's Most Prized & Favored Wines:
Cynthiana, $24.99
Cream Sherry, $19.99
Premium Champagne, $28.99
Fleur de Blanc, $12.99
(Plus thirty other offerings including a new Sauterne and American Port, three Sparkling Wines, a Burgundy, a Noah and a Vintage Merlot.)

Awards include: 2009 NJ Wine Growers Association Gold: Premium Chardonnay and Premium Champagne; Silver: Fresello, Burgundy, Merlot; and several Bronzes.

Harvest season: Varieties are harvested mid-September through early November.

Vineyard production: Forty acres containing thirteen varieties, including Baco Noir, Cabernet Franc, Cabernet Sauvignon, Cayuga, Chardonnay, Gewurztraminer, Merlot, Noah, Norton, Pinot Grigio, Riesling, Sauvignon Blanc, Vidal Blanc, and their own blueberries. All these produce 12,500 cases annually. All wines are from estate grown grapes.

Facility: Rightfully calling itself a winery resort, the expansive winery and tasting room includes a gift shop, several restaurants, a bake shop and deli, the Italianate Tuscany Hotel with each room individually designed, and a 7,200 golf course which hosts pro championships. Weddings and large meetings may be held in the Grand ball room (up to 280 people), the Burgundy Room (up to 150 people) or in party tents outside.

Directions: *From the Garden State Parkway,* take Exit 17 and turn left onto Route 50 North, then right onto Route 30. After two traffic lights, turn left onto Bremen Avenue (Route 674) and proceed 2.3 miles to winery.
From the North, Take Route 206 South, and make a right turn onto Route 30 East. Shortly, veer left onto Moss Mill Road, (Route 561 Alt.). Turn left onto Bremen Road and proceed 2.3 miles to winery.
From the South, you may take Route 54 North to the junction of Route 30 and take it East with a right turn.
From the Atlantic City Expressway, and the Shore, take Route 30 West to Bremen Avenue.

Part of the Hammonton Area Wine Trail, including Renault and Sylvin vineyards, and towards town, DiMatteo, Plagido's, and Tomasello vineyards.

SHARROTT WINERY

370 South Egg Harbor Road, (Rt. 561) Blue Anchor, NJ 08037
609-567-9463, lsharrott@sharrottwinery.com
www.sharrottwinery.com

Owners: Larry Sharrott Jr., Larry Sharrott, III, & wives Eileen Sharrott and Danielle Sharrott, respectively
Winemaker: Larry Sharrott, III

Public hours: *All year:* Wednesday–Sunday, 12ᴾᴹ–5ᴾᴹ, Fridays, 12ᴾᴹ–8ᴾᴹ. **($3 affords complete tastings and souvenir glass.)**

Events: The Riesling Release (lederhosen appreciated, but not required). Twice-monthly Live Music Series, out under the tents. Girls Night Out (LOMF). Grape Stomping with bare & purpled feet. Fall Festival, complete with hot air balloons and barbecue. Harvest Festival. Vineyard & winery tours available with winemaker most days.

Description: At last, a place to plunge in with both feet and trample out the new vintage with barrels of laughter. You might even win the Lucille Ball Look Alike Contest. With heavy finishes on fun, Larry Sharrott Senior and Larry Junior are creating world-competitive wines in the American tradition. Rising upslope to their family-built, no-pretense headquarters, visitors sense the freshness. The Sharrotts first planted vines in only 2004; created first vintage in 2007, and in 2008 (opening year) Sharrott Winery claimed its first world-class gold. Against 556 wineries from thirteen nations, judges of the Finger Lakes International Wine Competition gave top honors to their young, unoaked Chardonnay.
    The secret of Sharrott's success, insists Larry, is study and manure. Both father and son undertook the rigorous three-year viniculture/enology curriculum

at the University of California, Davis. They blended this West coast high wine tech with the American sustainability trend. Only pure Garden State pig and chicken manure fertilizes Sharrott grapes, and sprays are stingily employed. The results are distinctively full bodied Cabernet Franc, rich Shiraz, and deliciously balanced Vignoles.

Those favoring a picnic mode, may stroll out onto the wide tented patio with a glass of refreshingly sweet Crimson Sky (Sharrott's two-to-one best seller) and gaze down at the vineyard sloping away to the heavy forest. Note Sharrott's lush, shambling vines, less tightly manicured than the European style.

Come any time. But beware, Gents. Try to trespass on Sharrott's monthly "Ladies Night Out" and you'll be turned away.

Owner's most prized & favored wines:
Unoaked Chardonnay (2008 sold out, later vintages coming soon)
Vignoles 2008, $15.99
Riesling, $13.99
Cabernet Franc, $21.99
(Plus eleven other offerings including award winning Blueberry, Cabernet Franc Rosé, Sisu Vineyard Syrah, and their signature red blend, Crimson Sky.)

Awards include: 2009 Finger Lakes International Wine Competition: Best Chardonnay & Double Gold for Unoaked Chardonnay. 2009 Atlantic Seaboard Competition Silver: Barrel Reserve Chardonnay & Crimson Sky. 2008 New Jersey Growers Association Silver: Blueberry & Sisu Vineyard Syrah.

Harvest season: Varieties are harvested mid-September through mid-October.

Vineyard production: Six acres of vines containing Cabernet Franc, Chambourcin, Chardonnay, Syrah, and Vignoles varieties, which produce three-hundred cases annually. Up to forty percent of grapes purchased from other Garden State vineyards.

Facility: New tasting room accommodates thirty-five comfortably, with that many again spilling over into processing area for larger, jollier gatherings. Outside patio seats forty and may be shaded with party tents and umbrellas.

Directions: *Warning: GPS's often lead visitors astray. Check your map.*
From the Northwest, take I-295 South to exit 36A onto Route 73 South. Proceed 20 miles through Berlin center, and veer left onto Route 561 South (South Egg Harbor Road). Proceed one mile to winery on left.
From the NJ Turnpike: Take Exit 4 onto Route 73 South and proceed as above.
From Atlantic City Expressway, take Exit 31 to Route 73 North. Proceed 2.5 miles and turn right onto Route 561 South.
From Route 206 South, turn left onto Route 30 West (White Horse Pike). Turn left at Old Forks Road (see high school.) At Old Forks' end, turn right onto Route 561 North (South Egg Harbor Road). Winery is down on right.

Part of the Hammonton Area Wine Trail, including Amalthea, DiMatteo, Plagido, Sharrott, and Tomassello vineyards.

SILVER DECOY WINERY

610 Windsor-Perrineville Road, Robbinsvile, NJ 08691
609-371-6000, info@silverdecoywinery.com
www.silverdecoywinery.com

Owners: Todd Abrahams, Brian Carduner, Mark Carduner, Russell Forman, Jerry Watlington.
Winemaker: Mark Carduner

Public hours: *All year:* Fridays, 2^{PM} to 6^{PM}; Saturday & Sunday, 11^{AM} to 5^{PM}. **(Free complete tastings and tours.)**

Events: Tours daily. Their Hair of the Dog 5K Run & Pet Expo includes food, Silver Decoy wines, pet vendors, and, really and truly, a K9 Kissing Booth; (runners drink free). Traditional roast Pig Luau, complete with Balloon Bounce and acres of amusements. Fall Harvest Festival.

Description: Just a short cycle or drive from Central Jersey's high-tech and high-pressure business hubs, lies proof that the Garden State offers some competitively fine wines indeed. The old modest tasting room (and now its recently expanded version) buzzes with friendly, knowledgeable conversations. Mark Carduner, who for twenty-five years owned Carduner's Fine Wines and Spirits, explains the subtleties of taste and technique. His four fellow partners and many visitors add to the forum. Such expertise has born fruit. Within three years of its first planting, Silver Decoy was already winning state awards.

Yet guests find more than an enclave for the authoritative. The winery's name, as well as its 110 rural acres, hearken back to those predevelopment days when

---

many Mercer folks supplemented life with a little plowing and a little hunting. With this traditional, welcoming ease, the rolling green beyond the tasting room often sports fifty-foot tents and barbecue fires, set for frequent festivals. Join the five-hundred or so partiers at the 5k Rescue Run or the Hair of the Dog Festival—an excellent venue for their sweeter Ugly Duckling blends.

While visiting, don't miss taking a vineyard tour to catch a hint of Silver Decoy's success. The sixteen acres of clean, straight, immaculately leaf-pulled rows bespeak vigilant tending. Thus it has always been since 2001 when the partners set their first Cabernet Franc vines to earth. Today, their second-job adventure has blossomed into a full time quest for fine wine. Just sample the Cabernet Franc or the oaked Chardonnay and you'll appreciate their achievements.

Owner's most prized & favored wines:
Cabernet Franc 2007, $19.99
Sangiovese 2006, $35
Chardonnay, $14
Traminette, $14

(Plus nine other offerings including Retriever, a blend of Sangiovese and Cabernet; Raspberry, intriguing Ugly Duckling Red and White, and ten Marechal Foch, honoring the KC-10 flyers of McGuire Air Force Base.)

Awards include: 2007 New Jersey Winery of the Year; 2008 Gold: Raspberry; 2008 Wine Growers Association Gold: Cabernet Franc.

Harvest season: Varieties are harvested mid-September through early November.

Vineyard production: Sixteen acres of vines containing Cabernet Franc, Chambourcin, Chardonnay, Cayuga, Foch, Pinot Grigio, Merlot, Riesling, Syrah, Traminette, and Vignoles varieties, plus Raspberries. These produce nearly 2600 cases annually. Ninety percent of grapes come from Silver Decoy's estate. Two percent come from other Garden State vineyards.

Facility: Massive lawns and massive tents which host thousands may be all lighted up at night for an amazing effect. The modest tasting room has recently undergone expansion offering indoor accommodations for up to forty guests.

Directions: *From the New Jersey Turnpike* take Exit 8, following signs to Route 33 West (& Hightstown.) Take Route 33 West 1/4 mile, turn left as it joins Route 539. Proceed another 1/4 mile to Hightstown Diner, turning left onto Ward Street. Go 100 feet, turn right onto Route 539 (Main Street). After 1.5 miles, turn right onto Windsor-Perrineville Road. Winery is 1/4 mile on left.

From I-195, take Exit 8 (Hightstown) following signs to Route 539 North. Proceed 4 miles to traffic light, and turn left onto Windsor- Perrineville Road. Winery is 1/4 mile on left.

Part of the Central Jersey Wine Trail, including Cream Ridge, 4 JG's, Laurita, and Silver Decoy vineyards.

Swansea Vineyards

860 Main Street, Shiloh, NJ 08353
856-453-5778, info@swanseavineyards.com
www.swanseavineyards.com

Owner & Winemaker: Frank Baitinger III

Public hours: All year: Daylight Savings (April–October), Saturday & Sunday, 11^AM –6^PM;November–March, Saturday and Sunday, 12^PM–5 ^PM. **(Free tastings.)**

Events: Free tours of winery and vineyard during public hours. Harvest Celebration. Independence Day Summer Barbecue.

Description: Tucked between aged oaks, the Edwardian mansion of this business-like farm has welcomed visitors since 1828. You can almost feel the tradition as you walk the winding brick stairway, past the wrought iron furniture, and enter the family parlor which serves as the Swansea tasting room. Inside, manager Norma Maranzano has decoratively placed the hors d'oeuvres. (Don't forget to alternate sips of Serenity with chocolate.)

Owner, Frank Baitinger, who keeps himself more to the vineyard, may have granddaughter Courtney pouring Cygneture Red, from estate-grown Chambourcin. Or you may choose a glass of Swansong, a Baitinger original blended from seldom-used, flavorful Reliance and sweet Lakemont grapes.

Cumberland County's only commercial winery, Swansea was launched from a barrel of Chambourcin which Baitinger pressed at home in 2005, and, on a lark, entered in a Vermont contest. Spurred by the resulting medal, he and wife Shirley purchased the property and went fully commercial. The Swansea name harks back to the region's early settlers from Swansea, Wales who in 1663 discovered these fertile soils and called their farming town Shiloh, after the Biblical village of Hebrew sanctuary.

Today, the past carries forward. Picnicking from your seat beneath the shade trees, study the vintage farm tool collection of scythes, elder tractors, and bailing hooks. Past the white barns stroll out into a checkerboard of orchards and vineyards whose eighteen acres supply all Swansea's wines. Amidst this atmosphere, the winery's latest Ship John, a unique Cabernet blend, seems naturally appropriate. Hear the full story of this 1719 maritime wreck when you come to sample.

Owner's most prized & favored wines:
Ship John (a new red blend), $23
Chardonnay Reserve 2006, $22
Cygneture Red 2006, $9; later vintage, $18)
Serenity 2006, $12

(Plus twelve other offerings, including Swansong white, Kiwigold, and Spiced Apple. Many wines are offered in splits, including Peach and Nectarine.)

Awards include: 2006 Finger Lakes International Wine Competition Bronze: Chambourcin; 2008 Finger Lakes Bronze: Swansong and Cygneture Red; 2008 Eastern Wine International Competition Bronze: Chardonnay Reserve.

Harvest season: Varieties are harvested early September through early November.

Vineyard production: Twelve acres producing two-thousand cases annually. Some of the winery's grapes purchased from other Garden State vineyards.

Facility: Delightful tasting room, and larger party room behind which may accommodate up to twenty-five, all within the parlor of the old farm house. Picnic area outdoors overlooking vineyards, and party tents able to accommodate up to three-hundred on sprawling lawns.

Directions: *From Route 295 South,* exit onto Route 42 South and onto Route 55 South. Take exit 48 onto Route 641 South for seven miles to end, and turn left onto Route 77 South. Go four miles to Pole Tavern Circle, pick up 635 southwest toward Daretown and go eleven miles to end. Turn left onto Route 49 East. Go 1.5 miles to blinking light in Shiloh. Winery is 1/4 mile beyond on right.
From Garden State Parkway: Vineland, take Parkway Exit 36 to Route 40/322 West (Black Horse Pike), forking left onto 40 West (Harding Highway.) Follow Route 40 West through Mays Landing and turn left onto Old Landis Road just outside Vineland. Follow Landis Road several miles (or your favorite route) to Bridgeton. Pick up Route 49 West in Bridgeton and take it through Hopewell on into Shiloh. Pass the Fisher's Market, RottKamp Farms, and winery is just after on the left.
From Route 206 above Hammonton or Route 54 below it, head south until you meet Route 40 West, and proceed as above.

Often included in the Cape May Wine Trail, consisting of Cape May, Hawk Haven, Natali, Swansea, and Turdo Vineyards.

SYLVIN FARMS WINERY

24 North Vienna Avenue, Egg Harbor City, NJ 08215
609-965-1548, sylvinfarms@comcast.net
www.sylvinfarmswinery.com

Owner & Winemaker: Dr. Franklin Salek

Public hours: Please call ahead for tasting. **(Free tastings.)**

Events: Sylvin participates in all the Garden State Winegrowers festivals and events.

Description: "Cabernets are like an old man—slow gettin' up in the morning, but once up, they can go all day." Two lures will draw true wine lovers to the deep pinelands home/vineyard which Dr. Franklin Salek has tended for over three decades. Reason #1 sits on the plank atop two barrels in the modest room set aside for tasting. Some of the most robust, full-flavored wines found in this state, or beyond, stand here. Sip and agree with Frank, "This is Merlot as it should be." Those seeking a rich, masculine, no-gentility Cabernet Sauvignon, will want to make an arrangement. (Frank only makes "arrangements," not "appointments," for individual visitors to take tastings.)

Allure #2 is the arrow-sharp wine wisdom and historic tales stored within the man pouring at the bar. In 1976, Salek succumbed to "sheer madness," and with his wife Sylvia, launched his commercial vineyard. Believing his own research over conventional wisdom, Salek to this day fills his vineyard with all European vinifera varieties—no hybrids, no natives. Exceptional success has resulted. Today, Salek can cite startup stories about most Garden State wineries, many of whom began by buying his grapes. To hear these, ask for a vineyard tour and take along a glass of Sylvin's Italian-style Uva Accozzaglia, an annually changing field blend.

"You won't find sweet wines here," Salek explains patiently. Yet many's the white-Zinfandel lover converted to Sylvin's Sauvignon Blanc and Viognier. So after an afternoon at Renault Winery, continue briefly eastwards and enjoy a totally different, equally fruitful wine experience.

Owner's most prized & favored wines:
Sauvignon Blanc 2004, $13.99
Cabernet Franc 2004, $19.99
Uva Accozzaglia 2005, $14.99
Cabernet Sauvignon 1999, $19.99
(Plus twelve other offerings including a Sparkling Rkatziteli, and Sparkling Pinot Noir, a 2001 Merlot, and Sylvin's own Dolce Vino.)

Awards include: Sylvin began garnering New Jersey Governor's Cups in 1989 and now holds six of them. In various New Jersey Wine Growers Association Competitions, Sylvin's Cabernet Sauvignon has taken Silvers, while their Chardonnay, Sauvignon Blanc, and Sparkling Rkatziteli have earned Bronzes.

Harvest season: Varieties are harvested mid-September through mid-October.

Vineyard production: Eleven acres containing an unusual assortment of varieties, such as Barbara, Cabernet Franc, Cabernet Sauvignon, Corvina, Chardonnay, Dolcetto Merlot, Nebbiolo, Pinot Grigio, Pinot Noir, Rkatziteli, Sangiovese, Sauvignon Blanc, Semillion, Shiraz, Tempranillo, and Viognier. These produce nearly one-thousand cases annually all from Sylvin Farms grapes.

Facility: A personal, homey tasting room filled with lore, and literature makes for a memorable wine experience.

Directions: *From the North,* by your favorite method, get on Route 206 South and follow it towards Hammonton, turning left onto Route 30 East ((White Horse Pike). Shortly after, veer left onto Moss Mill Road (Alternate Route 561). Follow it across Route 563, and shortly past the "Renault Winery" sign, look for Vienna Avenue. The winery is a few hundred yards up on your right.

From the Garden State Parkway. South, getting off at Exit 44, take two immediate right turns onto Moss Mill Road (Alt. Route 561). Continue to Vienna Avenue and take it right.

From the South, by your favorite method, get onto Route 54 North heading up from Vineland. Passing through Hammonton, turn right on Route 30 West and proceed as above.

Part of a common Wine Trail including DiMatteo, Renault, and Sylvin Farms vineyards.

TERHUNE ORCHARDS

330 Cold Soil Road, Princeton, NJ 08540
(609-924-2310) info@terhuneorchards.com
www.terhuneorchards.com

Owners: Gary and Pam Mount
Winemakers: Gary and Tannwen Mount

Public hours: *All year:* Wednesday–Sunday, 12ᴾᴹ–5 ᴾᴹ. At the Farm Store bottles may be purchased year round, Monday–Friday, 9ᴬᴹ– 6ᴾᴹ; Saturday & Sunday, 9ᴬᴹ–5ᴾᴹ. **($5 affords complete tastings; $8 includes a souvenir glass.)**

Events: Too numerous to cover. A few include, Wassailing Party with dance, cheer & bonfire; Photo Contests; Pony Rides; Pick-your-own festivals from watermelons to blueberries—May through October; Puppet Theater (on Blueberry Bash weekend); Cider Squeezing Festival—with local music; Kite Flying Day; Summer Camp; September Scarecrow Music Festival; Bunny Chase (a springtime treasure hunt); Firefly Festival Barbecue; Pam's Freezing, Canning, and Preserving Class; Spinning Class; Pet & Learn Classes with farm animals; and many more.

Description: Conjure in your mind every fun and tasty aspect of the traditional family farm. Now imagine turning the kids loose in this bucolic oasis while you stroll along behind, swirling a glass of markedly full-bodied and just slightly sweet Vidal Blanc. Both the wine and the experience make up Terhune's.

　　Gary and Pam Mount and family manage the thirty-five crops on their two-hundred-acre retail farm where children come to work with animals; adults learn to spin, can, and prune; and everyone comes to select from the cornucopia of fresh produce. Every jar of jam is put up by Pam herself; and the tasting room's walnut bar was cut and polished by a family member.

Raised on a nearby farm, Gary married high school sweetheart Pam and served with her as Peace Corps agricultural agent in Micronesia. In 1975 they bought this fifty-five-acre plot from the Terhune family and have now quadrupled its size.

Returning home from her "California adventures," daughter Tannwen sensibly suggested, "Let's make wine." Thus, in 2005, hybrids were planted, with a 2009 initial harvest. Enjoy a glass of light, full-finish Chambourcin in the rustic tasting room for.

Owner's most prized & favored wines:
Vidal Blanc 2009, $17.50
Chardonnay 2009, $16.50
Barn Red 2009, $17.50
Apple Wine, $14.00
(Plus Terhune's Chambourcin, Cold Soil White, and Front Porch Breeze—a blend of Cayuga and Seyval.)

Awards include: 2010 New Jersey Wine Growers Association Bronze: Vidal Blanc.

Harvest season: Varieties are harvested early September through mid-October.

Vineyard production: Four-and-one-half acres containing primarily Cabernet Franc, Chambourcin Traminette, and Vidal varieties with some smaller sections of Cabernet Sauvignon, Chardonnay, Chardonel, Merlot, Riesling, and Sauvignon Blanc. Twenty percent of grapes were purchased from other Garden State vineyards this first year. That percentage will be cut to five in 2011 harvest and thereafter.

Facility: Charming 150-year-old barn serves as the cozy tasting room; a larger, nearby barn houses the farm market selling the farm's produce. Large parties use the vast barn or outside party tents. Groups from busloads to thousands can, and are accommodated. The Pick-Your-Own farm is on parallel Van Kirk Road. Many visitors lunch and stroll through nearby Rosedale Park.

Directions: *From the North.* take the NJ Turnpike to Exit 8 and follow signs for "Hightstown" and Route 33 West. Follow 33 West (Franklin Street) a short way into Hightstown where 33 turns left. Take the next right—Stockton Street—follow it across Route 130 where Stockton becomes Route 571, which you will follow 4 miles to Route 1. Turn left onto Route 1 South another 5 miles to I-95 South (different from the NJ Turnpike). Take I-95 1.5 miles to exit 7B, onto Route 206 North ("Lawrenceville-Princeton.") Turn left onto Cold Soil Road—fourth traffic light—and follow Cold Soil about 3 miles past Rosedale Park. The Winery is on the right shortly after the park.

From the South. Take Route I-295 North and cross Route 1 exit after which this interstate becomes I-95. Follow I-95 to exit 7B and proceed as above.

From Pennsylvania. Get onto I-95 North and exit onto 7B in New Jersey, and proceed as above.

Part of the Central Jersey Wine Trail, including Cream Ridge, Old York Cellars, Silver Decoy, Terhune, and Unionville Vineyards.

TOMASELLO WINERY

225 White Horse Pike Hammonton, NJ 0803
609-561-0567, wine@tomasellowinery.com
www.tomasellowinery.com

Owner & Winemakers: Charlie and Jack Tomasello

Public hours: *All year:* Thursday–Saturday, 9ᴬᴹ–7ᴾᴹ; Sunday, 11ᴬᴹ–6ᴾᴹ; Monday–Wednesday, 9 ᴬᴹ–6 ᴾᴹ. **(Free tastings.)**

Events: Tomasello's Opera Nights, held quarterly, (Feb., May, Oct., Dec.) in the 175-seat Vintner's Room offers guests a gourmet, locally prepared supper, each course paired with just the correct wine. Onstage, a troupe of Met-level professionals render favorite arias. Reserve for one, or subscribe to all four, early. It's always packed.

Description: It's a deceptively small white facade off Route 30, bearing the Tomasello name. But behind it lies the state's largest winemaker, pressing the greatest number of grape varieties (thirty-plus) which are sold in thirty-four states, Asia, and Canada. At the heart of this expanding business, which globally spreads the gospel of fine New Jersey wines, beats an aggressive striving for quality. And you reap the rewards.

Though true Jerseyphiles may prefer Tomasello's Sparkling Blueberry, wedding guests out in the Vintner's Room sipping their Blanc de Blanc Extra Dry, enjoy a competitively notable traditional Sparkling Wine. Specialist seekers after individual grapes will be impressed by the Nevers Oaked Cabernet Sauvignon and Petit Verdot. (These, plus Tomasello's Chardonnay, take their barrel fermentation in the subtle vanilla of French Nevers oak, while other varieties are more chocolate-enhanced by Kentucky barrels.)

Adventurous tasters may scan the forty-three-bottle wine list and sample a Pomegranate or American Almonique. Breaking the grapes' expected stereotype are Tomasello's refreshingly Dry Riesling and their fruitier Claret.

That day in 1933 when the "Noble Experiment" of Prohibition was repealed, berry and sweet potato farmer Frank Tomasello jumped in his truck and headed for Washington D.C. He returned with the 68th liquor-manufacturing license issued, and the family has made wine their sole careers ever since. Today, grand-sons Charlie and Jack take every advantage of their Outer Coastal Plain locale, experimenting with both French hybrids and American traditionals. Try the winery's unique night at the opera for critiquing the results—an elegant blend of magnificent arias, gourmet cuisine, and Tomasello's best.

Owner's most prized & favored wines:
> Nevers Oak Cabernet Sauvignon 2006, $30
> Petit Verdot 2006, $35
> Outer Coastal Plain Dry Riesling 2008, $13
> Sparkling Blueberry, $18

(Plus thirty-five other offerings, including Sparkling Wines, fruity Cranberry, Cherry, and Blackberry wines; the Russian grape Rkatsitelli; and three types of Chardonnay.

Awards include: Many state and international awards, including the 2007 Governor's Cup for Vidal Ice and Chambourcin. Also, in 2008, the Nevers Oak Cabernet Sauvignon 2006 was rated 93 by the Chicago Beverage Testing Institute.

Harvest season: Varieties are machine harvested in late August through mid-October. No harvest festival.

Vineyard production: Seventy acres with over thirty varieties in its own vine-yards, plus an enormous amount of locally purchased grapes makes this the Garden State's largest producer.

Facility: Ample tasting room. The Vintner's Room with stage seats 175 and is el-egantly set for weddings. Large party tents also are available for outdoor weddings.

Directions: *From the North,* By your favorite method get onto Route 206 South. Take it to the junction of Route 30 which is White Horse Pike. Turning right onto Route 30/White Horse, proceed .6 mile to traffic light. Winery is on right. (Route 206 South may be reached from Exit 7 on the NJ Turnpike.)

From the South, Take Route 54 North through Hammonton Township center, and turn left onto Route 30/White Horse Pike for .6 miles to winery on right.

From the Atlantic City Expressway, Take Exit 28 (Hammonton). Bear right off ramp onto Route 54 North and proceed as above.

Part of a common Hammonton Area Wine Trail, including Amalthea, DiMatteo, Plagido, and Tomasello vineyards.

TURDO VINEYARDS

3911 Bayshore Road, Cape May, NJ 08204
201-832-6955, luca@turdovineyards.com
www.turdovineyards.com

Owners: Salvatore, Sara, and Luca Turdo

Public hours: Memorial and Labor day, daily, 12ᴾᴹ–5 ᴾᴹ; off-season, Saturday & Sunday, 12ᴾᴹ–5ᴾᴹ; or call for appointment. **($5 tasting fee includes six wines and souvenir glass.)**

Events: Self-guided tours available during public hours. Free owner-guided tours upon availability. Walk amidst the wine and sea breezes.

Description: Now here's Italian! Undeterred by Bergen County's less than stellar soils, Salvatore and Sara Turdo had always made kitchen wine according to the traditions of their many preceding generations back in Sicily. Finally, in 1999 they purchased five-and-a-half sunny, Mediterranean-style acres in Cape May. By 2003, Turdo Vineyards' first fruits were pressed. True to the Old World way, no blends find their way into Turdo wines. Every weekend, son Luca with Sal and Sara drive the length of the Garden State—Bergen to Cape May—to lovingly tend their vines on the land they cleared by hand.

The result is a small but excellent array of full-bodied, single-grape vintages, each unfined and filtered. "We are as close to pure organic wine making and growing as you can achieve," notes Luca Turdo. "We employ only natural sulfites, and the result is no allergies for our customers." Good stewards of the earth, Turdo operates its entire growing and pressing process, and its facility by solar power. Several generations of Sicilian winemaking secrets comprise the Turdo success recipe, but Luca sums them up in "soul, climate, and passion."

It is easy to miss this iron gated winery amidst a seemingly suburban street. But don't. It is well worth your while to enter the homey atmosphere, enjoy a glass of Nero D'Avola (Sal's personal favorite), and imbibe the taste of European traditional quality.

Owners' most prized & favored wines:
> Nero D'Avola, $25
> Barbera, $25
> Nebbiolo, $25
> Sangiovese, $25

(Plus ten others all of which are Italian varietals. All grapes are Garden State.)

Awards include: 2009 Pacific Rim International Wine Competition Silver: Dolcetto and Nebbiolo; Bronze: Nero D'Avola. 2009 Indiana Wine Competition Double Gold: 2007 Barbera; Silver: 2006 Nebbiolo. 2009 NJ Wine Competition Gold: Barbera.

Harvest season: Varieties are harvested late August through early November.

Vineyard production: Five-and-one-half acres contain fourteen varieties, including the Nero D'Avola which is unique to this country. The vineyard produces one-thousand cases annually.

Facility: Cozy tasting room and sunny back porch.

Directions: *Head South on Garden State Parkway* South to it's end, turning onto Route 109, then 9 West. (109/9 is alternately called Sandman Boulevard & Ferry Road.) Turn left onto Bayshore Road. Proceed about a few blocks to #3911 on right.

Part of the Cape May Wine Trail, including Cape May, Hawk Haven, Natali, and Turdo vineyards.

UNIONVILLE VINEYARDS

9 Rocktown Road, Ringoes, NJ 08551
(908-788-0400) uvineyard@aol.com
www.unionvillevineyards.com

Winemaker: Cameron Stark; **Assistant winemaker:** Stephen Johnson

Public hours: *All year:* all week, 12ᴾᴹ–5 ᴾᴹ. **($5 affords five tastings from Classic series. $10 affords eight tastings from either Classic or Premium series.)**

Events: Free Cheese Tasting and Tour scheduled on weekends. Also, $35, two-hour in depth Bottle & Barrel Tasting Tour. Creating a wine blend for private groups under winemaker's supervision. Blind Tasting Challenge ($10). A Wine & Chocolate Affair in which participants create wine-infused truffles, $60. Individual Wine Release & Jazz Weekends. Music weekends from 20's to Swing to Current Rock. Grand Harvest Festival. Wine Tasting for Singles.

Description: Unionville in the Amwell Valley is historically a place of strong alliances. Revolutionary War buffs may recall that it was at Hunt House Farm General George Washington and Marquis de Lafayette joined in their 1778 Council of War, strategizing the Battle of Monmouth. Wine lovers will take a more tactile delight in the 2008 confederation that has united four local farms under the Unionville banner. Aided by accomplished winemaker Cameron Stark, Bob Wilson (owner of Pheasant Hill Vineyard, where Hunt House still stands), Zvi Erif, (owner of Amwell Ridge), and John and Lisa Hawkins (Bellwell Vineyards owners), recently purchased Unionville, providing over forty acres of total vines.

This has led to further unions, such as The Big O, a skillful marriage of Cabernet Franc and Cabernet Sauvignon—and Cam Jam, a lighter, yet equally complex Pinot Noir/Chambourcin blend.

From the loft of the 150-year-old restored barn that now serves as tasting room, sip a Chardonnay and look down on the glistening silver vats and tawny, arching barrels below. Part of Unionville's Single Vineyard series, the Pheasant Hill Chardonnay and Unionville Home Chardonnay remain segregated from vine to bottle. Each vat gets its own selected yeast. Each goes into its own type of old French oak barrel to best showcase its individual flavors.

From the tasting room, be sure to descend and explore the rolling lawns gracing Unonville's historic main house, built in 1858.

Peaches, apples, dairy, and now grapes, in turn, have thrived on this eighty-eight-acre farm. Choose your wine release weekend and enjoy this agricultural elegance.

Owner's most prized & favored wines:
Single Vineyard Chardonnays (Pheasant Hill, $45.95 or Unionville Home, $35.95)
The Big "O" 2007, $25.95
Mountain Road Pinot Noir, $35.95
Port, Vat 15, $25.95
(Plus sixteen other offerings including Lafayette's Pride, a dry Rosé; two dry Rieslings; and Cam Jam #1, an original red blend.)

Awards include: International Wine & Spirit Competition: 2010 Gold, Best in Class, Chardonnay; Critics' Choice International 2010 Gold: Revolutionary Red; 2009 San Diego Sommelier Challenge International. Gold: 2008 Pinot Noir; NJ Wine Growers Association Gold: Big "O" 2007; Silver: Chardonnay 2007 and Lafayette's Pride; Bronze: Pinot Noir.

Harvest season: Varieties are harvested early September through late October. Several Harvest Festivals.

Vineyard production: Four separate estates contribute to the forty-plus acres containing Cabernet Sauvignon, Chardonnay, Grenache, Mourvedre, Pinot Grigio, Pinot Noir, Rhone whites, Riesling, Syrah, and Viognier varieties. Together they produce five-thousand cases annually. A small percentage of grapes are purchased from other Garden State vineyards.

Facility: The cozy, warm upstairs tasting over looking the winery. The 1858, fieldstone Cave Room seats forty. Outdoor picnic area with tables and festival party tents host summer concerts with up to 150. Carefully tended flower gardens. The historic Hunt House adds history to the winery's charm.

Directions: *From Routes 202 & 31,* North or South, take the Wertsville Road Exit in Hunterdon County. Travel 2 miles, turn right onto Rocktown Road. Winery is first drive on left.

From Northern NJ Turnpike, take exit 14 onto I-78 West for 28.6 miles, to I-287 South towards Somerville. Exit I-287 onto Route 202/206 towards Princeton/Flemington. Proceed South 14.3 miles on 202 to Flemington. Go another 5.5 miles to Wertsville Road (Ringoes) and take jug handle crossover onto Wertsville Road, and proceed as above.

From Route 206. follow it north or south to the junction of Route 518, which you take west. Turn right at the second light, in downtown Hopewell, onto Greenwood Avenue (County 607) and go 4.6 miles to end. Turn left onto Wertsville Road and proceed as above.

Part of a common Central Jersey Wine Trail, including 4 JG's, Hopewell, and Unionville Vineyards. Also part of a West Central Wine Trail including Alba, Hopewell, Unionville, and Villa Milagro Vineyards.

VALENZANO WINERY

1090 Route 206, Shamong, NJ 08088. (Please note, the recent change of address from the old 1320 Old Indian Mills Road tasting room.)
(609-268-6731) tony@valenzanowine.com
www.valenzanowine.com

Owners: Anthony Valenzano Sr., Anthony Valenzano Jr., Mark Valenzano
Winemaker: Mark Valenzano

Public hours: *All year:* Wednesday & Friday, 11AM–5PM; Saturday & Sunday, 11AM–4M; or by appointment. **(Tastings are free with purchase of wine.)**

Events: Scheduled tours by appointment. Valenzano's is traditional host to the mid-September, two-day Winefest where ten-thousand people gather for New Jersey wines, food, music, local crafters, helicopter & pony rides—everything exciting.

Description: Neither the festive lights, nor the hospitality, nor the infectious smile of Big Al Oriente ever dims at Valenzano's warm stone and paneled tasting room. Ever since Tony Sr. passed around a little of his home made wine out the farmhouse's back door in the 1970's, the Valenzano's have earned a growing and devoted following. Visitors revel in the aura of homecoming, as Al guides their tastings through to a finale of Jersey Devil Port, a caressingly smooth blend of Cynthiana grapes and brandy, oaked for three years.
    Meanwhile, Tony Sr., and Jr., and son Mark blend labor and artistry in the vineyard and winery. Using their own forty-four acres and another two-hundred acres contracted from local farms, they keep a mindful balance between what suits both their Outer Coastal Plain conditions, and their customers' palates. Since the winery first officially opened in 1996, Valenzano's own Vitis-labrusca plantings (Concord and Niagara grapes) have thrived and pleased admirably. Wander the

gracefully curving walkways amidst the manicured Italianate gardens while sipping Valenzano's refreshingly full Chambourcin and you will also sense this match.

Those drawn to sweeter wines with a new twist must ask for the cleverly blended Pinelands Blush or rich Shamong Red. To sustain your trip to the gazebo, take a White Cabernet Franc or White Cranberry. In all Valenzano offerings, prices are kept to a minimum, making a great bargain for their maximal taste. To best take in the grand facilities, join the ten-thousand friendly folks at the September Winefest, where celebration covers every blade of grass.

Owner's most prized & favored wines:
Cynthiana 2002, $14.99 (Look for next vintage)
Red, White & Blueberry Sangria, $9.99
Old Indian Mills Blend, $16.99
Cabernet/Merlot, $9.99
(Plus fourteen other offerings, including a White Cranberry, Cranpagne, Jersey Devil Port, and White Cabernet.)

Awards include: Two Governor's cups in a row: Best American Varietal and Best Estate Grown Wine.

Harvest season: Varieties are harvested end of August through Late September.

Vineyard production: The forty-four Valenzano Farm's vineyard acres contain several varieties, including Cabernet Sauvignon, Cabernet Frank, Chardonnay, Cynthaniana, Merlot, Vidal Blanc. Using two-hundred contracted acres nearby for about seventy percent of their fruit, they produce 25,000 cases annually.

Facility: The old Shamong Road Wine House with its lovely Vintner's Pavilion gardens will still be in use for major banquets and houses groups of up to 175. However, Valenzano's new, greatly expanded Route 206 halls may even double that size. The larger, field stone and paneled tasting room easily hosts seventy five. Those wanting a more alfresco atmosphere, may rent the large party tent, with space for guests, stage, dance floor, and all the fun ingredients. Catering for all private events is also available.

Directions: *From the North,* Take Route 206 South, past the junction of Route 70, and continue to Tuckerton Avenue. About 2 miles down from Tuckerton, begin looking for the winery on your left.

From the South, Take Route 206 North up through Wharton State Park. Shortly after passing through Wharton and crossing Stores Road (Route 541) you will see the winery on the right.

From Route I-295, in western Jersey, Take Exit 34B onto Route 70 East to Route 206 South and proceed as above.

From Route 72, in eastern Jersey, follow it northwest to Route 70 West to Route 206 South.

Part of the popular Hammonton Area Wine Trail, including Amalthea, Plagido, Sharott, Tomasello, and Valenzano vineyards.

VENTIMIGLIA VINEYARD

101 Layton Road, Wantage, NJ 07641
973-875-4333, anne@ventivines.com
www.ventivines.com

Owner: Gene and Anne Ventimiglia
Winemaker: Gene Ventimiglia

Public hours: June–September, Weekends, 12ᴾᴹ–6 ᴾᴹ; October–December, weekends, 12ᴾᴹ–5 ᴾᴹ. **($5 affords complete tastings.)**

Events: None currently held during public hours, but plans are in the offing.

Description: High in their rocky, forested microclimate of New Jersey's Appalachians, the Ventimiglia family offers adventurous oenophiles both grapes and wines unique in our state. Spurred by a struggle to survive and thrive, this small, yet immensely varied vineyard displays an ever-evolving cycle of experimentation. To match their Rocky Ridge Farm's conditions, Gene, wife Anne, and son Anthony have filled their rows with cold-hardy Marquette, Leon Millot, and several Eastern European grapes.

    The challenge is constant. Chilling air breathes down the steep ridge, bearing killing frosts over the five acres of vines, well into mid-May. Mountain springs weave beneath the clay/stone soil, threatening root rot. But these vintners claim generations of tradition on their side. In 1900, Winemaker Eugenio Ventimiglia emigrated from Italy with a wealth of knowledge, passed onto grandson Gene.

Seeking to transform his hobby into a profession, Gene bought this land in 1996, and in 2006 the Vineyard opened. Two years later, the family had built the rustic tasting and processing rooms by hand.

Under Gene's eye, the cycle of experimentation continues into the winery. Employing an artistry of natural blending, Ventimiglia wines are all unfined and most, unfiltered. Be they estate grown, or from purchased grapes, such as Chardonnay or Merlot, look for that Ventimiglia hallmark—the soft finish. Such softness may be coaxed, as with the Cabernet Sauvignon's three years spent in costly Hungarian oak. Or it may lie in the selection of such rare grapes as the Spanish Carignane. Either way, come north and sip something new.

Owner's most prized & favored wines:
Chambourcin 2007, $18
Buon Giorno 2008, $14
Carignane 2006, $25
Cabernet Franc, $45

(Plus twelve other offerings, including such interesting blends as Fratelli Ventimiglia and Rocky Ridge Red, and newly released Syrah.)

Awards include: 2009 New Jersey Wine Growers Association Gold: 2007 Chambourcin; Bronze: Buon Giorno 2007 and Vidal 2007.

Harvest season: Through all September and October.

Vineyard production: Five acres of vines containing an ever- changing array of varieties, producing 830 cases annually. Up to ninety-five percent of grapes purchased from Garden State and other vineyards.

Facility: Rustic style tasting room filled with great hospitality, fellowship, and wine expertise.

Directions: *From the North (in New York),* Take I-84 East or West to Exit 1 onto Route 23 South, near the NJ/NY border. Follow Route 23 South through High Point State Park, then pass Route 519 and Sherman Ridge Road. Then after passing Wantage School Road on left, turn left onto Ryan Road. Fork left onto Layton Road. Proceed up hill, winery is on left.

From the South, from either east or west on Route I-80, exit onto Route 15 North (Exit 34). Take Route 15 North to Route 94 North, then turn left onto Route 23 North in Hamburg. From Route 23, turn right onto Ryan Road. Fork left onto Layton Road. Proceed up hill, winery is on left.

Part of the Sussex County Wine Trail, including Cava, Ventimiglia, and Westfall vineyards.

33 Warren Glen Road
Finesville, New Jersey 08865
908-995-2072

VILLA MILAGRO VINEYARDS

33 Warren Glen Road, Finesville, NJ 08865
908-995-2072, info@villamilagrovineyards.com
www.villamilagrovineyards.com

Owner: Steve & Audrey Gambino
Winemaker: Audrey Gambino

Public hours: *All year:* Saturday and Sunday, 12ᴾᴹ–6 ᴾᴹ; weekdays, by appointment. **($3 affords complete tastings and souvenir glass.)**

Events: Tours daily during public hours; also formal Wagon Tours of the property. Valentines Day Diner Dance (registration required.) Sunday Music Events. Wine Tasting Classes. Cooking Classes. Sunset Suppers. Dinner with the Chef for Culinary Club members. Full Strawberry Moon (in June) Event.

Description: It somehow seems fitting that this truly organic winery should take its setting along the pristine, forested palisades overlooking the Delaware River, just below the Water Gap. Steve and Audrey Gambino bought their farm in 2001 with a winery in mind. But before planting, they spent two years resting and purifying the soils with a strict organic regimen. Ask about their detoxifying pre-vine plantings.

By 2005, Milagro harvested such varieties as Cabernet Sauvignon, Chardonnay, and Pinot Grigio commonly suited to their Bordeaux-style Warren Hills Region. They also brought to press the less typical Malbec, Norton, and Shiraz. The result has fed five distinct blends, minimally aged two years each, that signify this winemaker's imagination and skill. The full Villa Milagro experience may best be achieved by filling a glass with the newly released Rubia, and relaxing in a rocker out on the Gambino's spacious back porch in autumn. The widely spaced vines slant sharply toward the Delaware where trees of brilliant hues rain down leaves upon the dark waters.

Come for the Sunset Suppers and you just may witness Steve atop his home made flame-throwing tractor. This ultimate boy's-toy weed killer wanders the nine-foot row spacings which were designed more to accommodate extra sun than machinery.

Many claim they can taste the difference in fruit from vines fertilized by naught but local manure and other organics. To learn the benefits, try taking one of Milagro's wine tasting classes, or a specialized cooking class taught by noted nutritionist Dr. Audrey Cross. Healthier vistas opened on food, wine, and life.

Owner's most prized & favored wines:
Rubia 2006, $12.99
Dos Luz, $17.99
Roja Dulce, $14.99
Suave, $21.99
Sombra, $18.99
(All are Milagro's own special blends)

Harvest season: Varieties are harvested mid-September through late October.

Vineyard production: Eleven acres of vines containing Chardonnay, Cabernet Franc, Cabernet Sauvignon, Frontenac, Malbec, Norton, Pinot Grigio, Sangiovese, Syrah, and Vidal varieties, producing 650 cases annually. All wines come from Villa Milagro grapes.

Facility: A grand back porch affording a sweeping view of the vineyard and Delaware River. Tasting room offers view into processing room. Hiking trails abound in this area. Large party tent for events.

Directions: Warning, *GPS tends to get confused on this one.*
Scenically from South, by your favorite Route (e.g. interstates 95 or 1-95) get onto Route 29 North to its end in Frenchtown. Turn left at "T," then first right onto Harrison Street. Proceed into Milford, turning left at light, then next right (Church Street) which curves and becomes Route 627. Winery is 6.3 miles up. See their barn, turn right then immediate left—See sign and #33 mailbox.
From North, get onto I-78 West (e.g. via 287). Taking Exit 4 (Stewartsville) turn left off ramp onto Route 637 (Main Street). At "T" junction, turn right onto Route 639 (Warren Glen-Reigelsville Road and go 2.8 miles. Bear left onto Route 519. Proceed 4 miles as the road becomes Route 627, then see mailbox #33 and winery sign.

Part of the Wine Train from Philipsburg and a bus tour linking Villa Milagro with Alba Vineyard.

WAGONHOUSE WINERY

183 Cedar Road, Mickleton, NJ 08056
609-780-8019, inquire@wagonhousewinery.com
www.wagonhousewinery.com

Owners: Daniel & Heather Brown
Winemaker: Daniel Brown

Public hours: Winery currently not open to public. See website for a farm market near you carrying Wagonhouse wines. For purchases, and delivery options call for an appointment, or e-mail orders@wagonhousewinery.com

Events: No events at farm, however visit the website for the several liquor stores and area farm markets which sell and celebrate Wagonhouse wine.

Description: Wagonhouse epitomizes classic farm hospitality. No fancy tasting room—YET. Just a fascinating homestead with busy, yet friendly folks who will gladly walk you around their lovingly tended acreage.

Here is a family farm that has grown it all. Since Richard S. Brown bought the original 106 acres in 1890, to the 2,500 acres worked five generations later, cows, chickens, hay, grain, fruits, and, as of 2004, grapes, have graced their fields. From such young vines, Daniel and wife Heather Brown have produced a selection of sumptuous, full-bodied varietals. Pick up a bottle of their crisp Cabernet

---

Garden State Wineries Guide

Sauvignon or smooth Chardonnay to bring home and share with your favorite wine accomplice.

Dan Brown stands with the many winemakers who believe the key to fine wine lies in the field. And, like others, the way he draws out these optimum flavors are markedly individual. A professional soil conservationist, he has engineered an eco-friendly, integrated pest control, whose chronological precision places less chemicals onto fruit, and into roots. Part of this system is a Daniel Brown original, jerry-rigged sprayer with flanging tractor nozzles which hit grape clusters from all sides. An invention to behold. Additionally, Brown has designed watering system which rations timely nourishment into his sandy, Outer Coastal Plain soils.

Those seeking sweeter blends, might try the Fallen Quaker red. Fruit wine lovers should experiment with Wagonhouse's Sundance Peach, and Ornery Apple. Call or e-mail for pick up directions and a list of nearby outlets. The taste is definitely worth the trip.

Owner's most prized & favored wines:
Cabernet Sauvignon, $11.99
Merlot, $11.99
Chardonnay, $11.99
Pinot Gris 2007, $11.99

(Plus five other offerings including three fruit wines, and their new Cabernet Franc and Sangiovese. Also, look for upcoming Strawberry and four other new blends this Fall 2010.)

Awards include: 2008 New Jersey Wine Growers Association Silver: Cabernet Sauvignon; Bronzes: Blueberry, Peach, Pinot Gris.

Harvest season: Varieties are harvested early September through late October.

Vineyard production: Three and one-half acres containing Cabernet Sauvignon, Chardonnay, Pinot Gris, and Sangiovese varieties. These produce 1,700 cases annually. All of the grapes used are grown on the estate. Fruits for fruit wines are purchased from Garden State farms.

Facility: No tasting room on site, but warm hospitality.

Directions: From the NJ Turnpike, take Exit 2 onto Route 322 Southeast (Swedesboro Road). Turn left onto Route 45 (North Main Street), then turn left onto Cohawkin Road. After a short ways, fork left onto Cedar Road. After a few hundred yards, look for the winery's unpaved driveway on left.
From Central Jersey North or South, get onto Route 55 and take it to Route 322. Turn onto Route 322 West, then right onto Route 45 North and proceed as above.

Part of the Glouster County Wine Trail, including Cedarvale, Heritage, and Wagonhouse vineyards.

WESTFALL WINERY

141 Clove Road, Montague, NJ 07827
973-293-3428, westfallwinery@gmail.com
www.westfallwinery.com

Owner: Loren & Georgene Mortimer
Winemakers: Loren & Georgene Mortimer

Public hours: April–November: weekends, 12 PM–5 PM. Special Valentines Weekend opening. **(Free tastings.)**

Events: Free tours daily during public hours. The Great Chili Cookoff where over seven-hundred guests sample & vote (August). Fathers' Day Pig Roast. May Barrel Tasting ($5). Independence Day Barbecue. Louisiana Blues Barbecue with spicy Cajun foods and bands to match.

Description: Turning off the narrow, wooded road into New Jersey's northern-most winery, you'll feel you have stepped back into some grand historic piece of bucolic history. And you have. Before there was an America, Simon Westfall purchased this farmland from England's Earl of Perth. Ever since, the farm has played its part in our nation's historic events.

Today, Westfall's broad compound of substantial red, framed barns amidst still ponds and well grazed pastures, present an idyllic backdrop for tasting Loren and Georgene Mortimer's sumptuously blended wines. The three acres of onsite vines are supplemented by meticulous grape selections from Italy, Chile, Argentina, the Rhine region, and New York's Finger Lakes.

The result is a roster of gold medal blends such as the Rhone Blend and popular Vino Russo. Lovers of the elusive Malbec will discover a hearty version rivaling any Argentinean import.

In a match made for wine, Loren and Georgene met and wed at the vineyard-rich surroundings of New York's Ithaca College. Georgene dowered an Italian family tradition of wine making, and an environmental science Ph.D. with organic chemistry expertise. Loren contributed his own viniculture skills and a family mastery of food and agriculture. It was Loren's grandfather Charles Mortimer, former president of General Foods Corporation, who purchased and renovated Westfall farm in 1940. In 2002, they founded Westfall, and later their South Carolinian Island Winery.

Whether you visit during Westfall's Father's Day Pig Roast or famed Chili Cookoff, bring the family. While the children explore the stables and pens, you might explore MidSummer White, a creative blending of Seval Blanc, Traminette, and Cayuga White.

Owner's Most Prized & Favored Wines:
Spanish Passion (Sangria), $15
Rhone Blend, $18
Nebbiolo (new), $20
Apple Cinnamon (New, all Jersey apples), $15
(Plus eighteen other offerings including Meritage, Peach Chardonnay, and their popular Cranberry.)

Awards include: 2009 New Jersey Wine Growers Association Gold: Rhone and Vino Rosso Reserve.

Harvest season: Varieties are harvested mid-September through mid-October.

Vineyard production: Three acres containing Concord, Niagara, and Traminette varieties. Together with select grapes imported from as far away as Chile, the winery produces seven-thousand cases annually.

Facility: Full-size farm style tasting room, a working farm to explore, rolling grassy lawns with party tents to host such events as the pig roasts and chili cookoff.

Directions: By your favorite route, take yourself to the northwestern tip of New Jersey. This may entail:

From Route 80 West, take Exit 34B, onto Route 15 North, which after several miles merges left onto Route 206 North. Follow Route 206 several miles to Montague. Here turn right onto Clove Road, and proceed five miles to the winery.

From Route 23 North, follow Route 23 into Montague, turn left onto Clove Road. Winery is three miles on your right. Route 23 is also accessible from I-84 East or West.

Part of the Sussex County Wine Trail, including Cava, Ventimiglia, and Westfall vineyards.

NOTES

GARDEN STATE WINE GRAPES GUIDE
POPULARLY GROWN RED AND WHITE WINE GRAPES

Barbera
Cabernet Franc
Cabernet Sauvignon
Catawba
Cayuga
Chancellor
Chardonnay
Chambourcin
Concord
Corvina
Cynthiana (synonym, Norton)
Dechaunac
Dolcetto
Marechal Foch
Fredonia
Gewurztraminer
Ives
Lemberger

Leon Millot
Malbec
Marquette
Merlot
Nebbiolo
Nero D'Avola
Niagara
Noah
Norton (synonym, Cynthiana)
Petit Verdot
Pinot Grigio (Pinot Gris)
Pinot Noir
Rkatsiteli
Riesling
Sangiovese
Sauvignon Blanc
Semillon (not common)

Syrah
Seyval Blanc
Traminette
Tempranillo (not common)
Uva Accozzaglia
Viognier
Vidal
Zinfandel
Zweigelt (not common)

(Prepared by Anthony Fisher, former Regional Vice President of the American Wine Association; and Gary Pavlis, former President, American Wine Association.

GARDEN STATE WINE ASSOCIATIONS, SHOPS, AND EDUCATIONAL RESOURCES

HELPFUL ASSOCIATIONS

Garden State Winegrowers Association
(609-588-0085) wineinfo@newjerseywines.com, www.newjerseywines.com.
The Winegrowers Association is the mainstay of the state's wine community.
Check out their numerous huge festivals around the state - an ideal way to get a
full sampling of Garden State vintages.

Outer Coastal Plain Vineyard Association
www.outercoastalplain.com, info@outercoastalplain.com.

STORES

There are countless wine stores around the Garden State, but a few of our favorites are:

Annata Wine Bar
216 St., Hammonton, NJ 08037 (609-704-9797) or 1-877-7ANNATA, www.an-
natawinebar.com
    Located in Hammonton, it the hub of more than half a dozen wineries, An-
nata stocks many of this state's, and other lands' finest. Here's your chance to
sample and compare, while pairing with excellent food.

Joe Canal's Discount Liquors
Stores may be found in Bellmawr, Delran, Egg Harbor, Hammonton, Iselin
(Woodbridge) Lawrenceville, Marlton, Millville, Rio Grande, Sicklerville, and West
Deptford. For addresses of these 11 New Jersey Stores visit www.joecanals.com.
    Before opening his own store renowned wine expert Anthony Fisher served
as Canal's sommelier and built a fine collection which has only improved with
age. Selection is wide and prices are very competitive. (609-520-0008)

The Bottle Barn

65 West Broad St., Gibbstown, NJ 08027 (856-423-3608).

Owner, Anthony Fisher stands as one of the Garden State's foremost wine judges and educators. He is a certified wine judge, member of the Dionysian Society and former regional vice-president of the American Wine Society. (Read his "Taster's Guide" and "Evaluation Chart" in this volume's introduction.) His store's selection reflects his exquisite, broad ranging taste at affordable prices. Check website for his not-to-be-missed classes.

GETTING YOUR FEET WET

The schools and wine works below offer would-be winemakers the chance to come individually or in groups and actually press and produce wine under the supervision of qualified instructors. Typically these shops supply all the equipment, and most supply the grapes. You just bring your enthusiasm and ideas for a personal label.

One caveat—most of these shops are open seasonally, typically right after the late summer and fall harvest. Be sure to check ahead.

Bacchus Winemaking Club
1540 Route 37, West Toms River, NJ 08755, (732-505-6930)
www.bacchusnj

Coda Rossa's Winery
The Wine Room of Cherry Hill
1 Esterbrook Lane, Cherry Hill, NJ 08003, (856-424-9463), www.thewineroom.com

The Brewers Apprentice
865 Business Route 33 West, Freehold, NJ 07728, (732-863-9411), www.brewapp.com, (Beware: many GPS steer you away from the business route 33.)

California Wineworks
476 Route 17 North, Ramsey, NJ 07446, (201-785-9463), www.cawineworks.com.

Grape Beginnings Wine School
31 NcKeab St. Freehold, NJ 07728, (732-431-3313), www.time4goodwine.com.

The Grape Escape
12 Stults Road, Suite 101, Dayton NJ 08810, (609-409-9463) www.thegrapeescape.net.

Make Wine with Us
21 Currie Ave., Wallington, NJ 07057, 201-876-9463, www.makewinewithus.com.

The Wine Makers Cellar
1050 Goffle R., Hawthorne, NJ, (973-238-1400), www.thewinemakerscellar.com. Tours available, hours by appointment only.

Winemakers of Somerset

12 Church St., Bound Brook, NJ 08805, (www.njwinemakers.com.)

Vintner's Circle

Four New Jersey Locations: Andover (973-940-7348), Hackettstown (908-979-0700), Middletown (732-671-5200), and Whippany (973-585-4719), www.vintnerscircle. com.

NON-FARM WINERIES

Balic Winery

6623 Harding Hwy. (Route 40), Mays Landing NJ 08330, (609-625-2166); www. balicwinery.com.

Entering its fifth decade, Balic offers a wide variety of dry, demi-sec, and berry wines from imported grapes and juice.

CLASSES & TEACHERS

Gary Pavlis' Rutgers University Courses

The truth is, anywhere Gary Pavlis is giving a wine course, you want to travel there, taste, and learn. But his open courses at his home base of Rutgers University in New Brunswick, where he serves as professor and agricultural agent, are ideal. Professor Pavlis typically assembles several winemakers and experts to help in the class, including one of our favorites, Dr. Lena Brattsten, who also teaches an excellent wine appreciation course at Rutgers.

The Educated Grape

203 Main St., #259 Flemington, NJ 08822, (973-699-2199), www.theeducatedgrape. com. Owner and educator George Staikos sets up tastings and classes for wine and food pairing in your home or favorite restaurant.

International Wine Center

350 7th Ave (between 29 & 30th sts.) New York, NY, www.internatoinalwine-center.com

When you finally get truly serious about wine, and perhaps are considering an oenophilic career move, the Wine Center is the place to come take your training. Every bit worth the Big Apple pilgrimage, their instructors are of the highest quality. At the same time, we like the sensible approach of instructors like Steve Miller, DWS, CWE, who buys for the highest-end markets, yet annually publishes his list of low-price Reds and Whites.

Wine Events

www.localwineevents.com, (610-647-4888).

An excellent website and newsletter for keeping up with what's happening in wineries and the wine world in New York, Pennsylvania, and New Jersey.

Wine Making Supplies & Accessories

Gary's Wine Marketplace
Stores in Bernardsville (908-766-6699), Madison (973-822-0200), and Wayne (973-633-3900). Visit www.garyswine.com.

In addition to an impressive selection of wines, Gary's offers a delightful assemblage of wine accessories from delicate glass charms to bottle and barrel cages.

Oceans of Wine Supply, Inc.
1540 Route 37 West, Toms River, NJ 08755, (732-240-4993).

Princeton Homebrew
208 Sanhickan Drive, Trenton, NJ, (609-252-1800).

EPILOGUE
THE IMPORTANCE OF WINE IN THE GARDEN STATE

Congratulations for compiling this guide to showcase New Jersey's wineries. After reading through this guide and beginning to explore the wide array of wineries, consumers will see that New Jersey is a fabulous source for fine wines, comparable to wines produced in the top wine regions in the world. In fact, some New Jersey wines have won international awards for taste and quality, outscoring French and California entries.

The wine industry is a vital part of what makes New Jersey the Garden State. New Jersey is uniquely suited for wine grape production. Our vintners grow a wide variety of grapes, such as Chardonnay, Chambourcin, Riesling, Vidal Blanc, Cabernet Franc, Cabernet Sauvignon, and Merlot, and fruits, such as raspberry, blueberry and cranberry, for sweeter dessert wines.

There are three regions federally designated as American Viticultural Areas in New Jersey. The largest of those regions – the Outer Coastal Plain in the southern part of the state – is known for its microclimate, with sandy, well-drained deep soils, milder winters and a good deal of sunshine, similar to Bordeaux and Burgundy in France.

New Jersey's wine industry is growing every year. In the 2007 United States Census of Agriculture, there were seventy-nine farms harvesting 952 acres of grapes, with a market value of $4.7 million. In 2008, there were 282,421 taxable gallons reported sold by New Jersey wine producers.

Aside from producing interesting and tasty wines, New Jersey's wineries also invite the public on to their farms to experience life in the vineyard, learn about wine-making and grape growing and take a step back in time in an old world atmosphere. Some wineries have wine-tastings, concerts, dinners and even barefoot grape stompings. Several even host your special events, such as weddings. These winery experiences can provide people with lasting memories.

Many of New Jersey's wineries produce wine made one-hundred percent with their own grapes and fruit, or those purchased from local farmers. When drinking a glass of New Jersey wine or visiting a winery, you are supporting our agricultural industry and helping New Jersey remain the Garden State.

Sincerely,

Douglas H. Fisher
New Jersey Secretary of Agriculture

NOTES

INDEX

Traminette 31, 39, 45, 47, 55, 57,
    79, 85, 101, 104
Trenton 2, 32, 53, 108
Turdo Vineyards 13, 24, 88–89
Turdo Vineyards on Wine Trail
    69, 81

U

Unionville Vineyards 13, 65,
    90–91
Unionville Vineyards on Wine
    Trail 65, 71, 85, 91
Uva Accozzaglia 83, 104

V

Valenzano Winery 14, 92–93
Ventimiglia Vineyard 14, 94–95
Vernon, Dr. Dan xi

Vidal 37, 41, 51, 57, 59, 65, 71, 73, 75,
    84, 85, 87, 93, 95, 97, 104, 109
Villa Milagro Vineyards 14, 35,
    96–97
Villa Milagro Vineyards on Wine
    Trail 33, 41, 59, 91
Viognier 17, 35, 39, 83, 91, 104

W

Wagonhouse Winery 14, 98–99
Warren County 18
Warren County Wine Trail 33
Warren Hills Wine Trail 59
Westfall Winery 14, 41, 100

Z

Zinfandel 45, 83, iv
Zweigelt 67, 104

NOTES

NOTES

NOTES

NOTES

WINE BOOK PUBLISHER OF THE YEAR

Gourmand World Book Awards, 2004

The Wine Appreciation Guild has been an educational pioneer in our fascinating community.

—Robert Mondavi

Your opinion matters to us…

You may not think it, but customer input is important to the ultimate quality of any revised work or second edition. We invite and appreciate any comments you may have. And by registering your WAG book you are enrolled to receive prepublication discounts, special offers, or alerts to various wine events, only available to registered members.

As your first bonus for registering you will receive, free of charge, our bestsell-

- Wine regions
- The process: from grapes to glass
- Enjoying wine: rituals and tasting
- Wine Guide, a fascinating database for choosing different wines
- Cellar Log Book, that will allow you to document your own wine collection.

YOU CAN REGISTER YOUR BOOK BY:

Phone: (800) 231-9463
Fax: (650) 866-3513
Email: Info@WineAppreciation.com

Or snail mail the form on the following page:

REGISTRATION CARD
for GARDEN STATE WINERIES

Name_____Date_____

Professional Affiliation_____

Address_____

_____

City_____State_____Zip_____

E-Mail_____

How did you discover this book?_____

_____

Where did you acquire this book?_____

_____

Was it a good read? (circle)   Poor   1   2   3   Excellent

Suggestions_____

_____

_____

_____

Comments_____

_____

_____

_____

_____

_____

You can register your book by phone: (800) 231-9463; Fax: (650) 866-3513;
Email: Info@WineAppreciation.com; or snail mail.

THE WINE APPRECIATION GUILD

360 Swift Avenue
South San Francisco, CA 94080

www.wineappreciation.com

Fold Here ▲

Tape Closed Here ▼